SOLVING THE DAM PUZZLE

99 Ways Digital Asset Management Initiatives Fail and Best Practices for Success

by Dan McGraw

Blurb Publishers
San Francisco California

Library of Congress Cataloging-in-Publication Data applied for.
Dan McGraw/books@solvingthedampuzzle.com

Ordering Information:
Quantity sales. Special discounts are available on quantity purchases by corporations, associations, and others.
For details, contact books@solvingthedampuzzle.com

Solving the DAM Puzzle/ Dan McGraw. —1st ed.

SOLVING THE DAM PUZZLE

99 Ways Digital Asset Management Initiatives Fail and Best Practices for Success

by Dan McGraw

Blurb Publishers
San Francisco California

CONTENTS

This book is dedicated to my three favorite puzzlemasters Shane, Sarah and Shannon with all my love

"Sometimes the hardest pieces of a puzzle to assemble, are the ones missing from the box."
- Dixie Waters, Author

"If content is king, he has a pretty lousy castle"
- Television Network VP of Technology

PREFACE

Whether I'm at a movie studio, a museum, or a small truck parts manufacturer in upstate Michigan, I see and hear of Digital Asset Management or "DAM" puzzles. Although some of the pieces to these puzzle are technical in nature, the bad news is the problem is usually in the "space between the keyboard and the chair." We create our own puzzles with the way we think, work and use resources. Technology has become the standard answer to most business issues. The good news however, is the solution is not technology, it's people.

Marketing departments, production teams, IT departments, legal staff, executives and other professionals struggle with DAM puzzles in both obvious and subtle ways. They work in environments where poor processes, outdated organizational methods, financial policies, crudely evolving technology platforms, and wrong applications limit them, which erodes profitability. It's difficult or sometimes even impossible for these professionals to do the jobs they are paid to do without continually increasing costs, resorting to complex work arounds or reducing outputs. They live in a digital world but work in analog paradigms that are difficult to overcome. Any company looking to survive in the next five years must undergo a dramatic digital shift. DAM, the heart of that change, is often ignored or overlooked.

Against this backdrop, I've witnessed companies lose market share and key performers, others that can't activate marketing fast enough, and some who are sucked into copyright infringement lawsuits. I've seen managers blame their staff and staff begging management to provide more help, tools or hard drives.

As digital media pours in, I see everyone doing whatever he or she can to keep his or her head down and survive. In many ways, they know the puzzle exists, but have neither a reference picture nor the knowledge to solve it. Like barbarians at the gate, the digital revolution stormed in, and all but a few were defenseless or unaware. How digital asset management could possibly offer improvements in profitability, let alone inaugurate a digital shift, was a mystery to them. Instead, they took organic approaches to managing media with cheap solutions that cost them dearly.

Some held to traditional IT approaches. A Chief Information Officer for a very large insurance firm considered his knowledge sufficient to figure it out. “They are just files, what’s the big deal?”

He had never heard of DAM and his only experience with media files was storing and securing them. He even challenged me on the very existence of DAM as a legitimate industry. SharePoint, he said, was “magic compared to hard drives” and therefore his optimal choice. His approach is not unique.

Some think it’s best handled by adding more staff, contractors, hard drives or by purchasing applications from well known brand names. One of today’s top vendors is conducting one of the most misleading product shell games I’ve ever seen in the DAM industry. By the time well intentioned marketing teams purchase it, its too late.

I see other teams, armed with any conceivable budget, wide vendor options, short on awareness and long on desperation, make knee-jerk reactive purchases. These are smart, creative and well-educated people looking for clues and answers from technology vendors to stop the digital bleeding. Vendors are all too happy to oblige and before long everyone is in a sales demo. When a business takes that simple step, without the knowledge of best practices, experience in DAM, or a legitimate business case, the same frustrating and expensive progression begins. After several years of engagements and hundreds of educational workshops, conference panels, webinars and countless calls and meetings, I found I was having the same conversation about fundamental DAM strategy and implementation practices over and over. Even though DAM is no longer a nascent field, people still stumble onward without fundamental knowledge.

My passion is unlocking creativity and business value by looking to overcome the technology hurdles. I grew up making movies, learning about electronics and photography, and eventually worked in film, 3D animation, media technology, and then accidentally stumbled into DAM. Like many others, I discovered I was working in the DAM field long before I had even heard the term.

I have been on all sides of the DAM equation: user, developer, strategist, vendor and educator. In all of these roles, I didn't look to be the smartest guy in the room, but hopefully, the most helpful for enabling success with technology and people. As a Digital Asset Management consultant, I believe that regardless of your role in creative media production, IT, middle or C-level management, finance or content delivery, an understanding of

DAM concepts will prove not only invaluable, but also profitable. It may even initiate a renewed vision for a struggling enterprise.

The purpose of this book is to bring relevant concepts and experiences to those solving their own "DAM puzzles" during the early stages through implementation. I'll draw you a "big picture" of DAM, as I've done for many others. While there are other fine books on DAM by experts such as David Diamond, David Austerberry, and Elizabeth Ferguson Keathley, here you'll get my own perspective on the "why" and the "what" that has worked or undermined a DAM initiative.

Whether you are planning to solve a DAM puzzle for creative services, marketing, or operations, this book can be a guide if only to know how DAM puzzle pieces should fit. My hope is that you'll develop a foundation and come to understand how DAM is more than turning to vendors, loading software on a server, handing the reins over to a tech team or uploading media to a cloud site. Through examples, I'll explain what I consider to be the basics, best practices, and offer many examples of what not to do and why. You'll learn how to deal with vendors of DAM systems, unlock new ways to save money, increase sales, and inaugurate a legitimate digital media strategy for your growing organization. You'll also understand how to build a business case for DAM.

If you're looking for help to manage or improve an existing DAM strategy or technology, you'll have your own experience to reflect on. You'll see where your project tracked with recommended practices, and where it didn't. I'd love to hear your own story.

DAM is fraught with a multitude of puzzle pieces, including media formats, metadata, technology, costs, users, and agendas—which all have to fit together. Don't be discouraged. In this book, you'll see why success is achieved when the pieces lock together, areas of concern and why others failed. However small or large your DAM puzzle is initially, after your stakeholders accept the vision and users adopt technical platforms, your organization can evolve from the toil of survival to new level of business renewal and innovation. It will be worth it.

This book covers many areas, but it is by no means as exhaustive as it could be. The permutations that result from DAM initiatives are so vast, it would be impossible to cover them all. I'll include and discuss some technical terms (and provide a definition for them), but this book is not about technology.

Today, we can use technology to do nearly anything and sometimes the problem is having too much of it. In most instances, many cheap solutions create expensive chaos. I seek to uncover the important principles to keep your initiative on track for good, help you to recognize and determine the right direction, and avoid expensive surprises.

I'll likely leave out some areas that you'll want to discuss. I'm happy to take your feedback and cover it in another form. Until then, I wish you all success in solving your own DAM puzzle!

Dan McGraw
danmcgraw@me.com
Washington DC, Spring 2016

"Oh, we're good. We put everything on DropBox."
- Senior Director for top clothing brand

1 WHAT'S YOUR DAM PUZZLE?

Digital Asset Management

DAM. It can be a bewildering topic for the novice, over simplified by executives, and ever changing for the veteran. It's a term that doesn't mean just one thing. Some use it as a catchall phrase for any database that manages media related information or the actual digital files, and for others, a place to store graphics, photos and video as an archive. Still others use the term to refer to an industry or a module within a larger content management application. And some simply consider it a subject they've heard about, but don't understand or have tried to forget. Why is this the case? What is it about DAM that makes it such a puzzle?

To start, let's open the box with some history…

The Analog World

In the 1960's, nearly everything was analog. From the business side, the fruit of an average knowledge worker's labor would be accomplished within or result in a physical form. Typewriters pounded out letters or contracts. Copies of documents were made using messy carbon paper. Regular stamped mail couriered all documents and slide rules did calculations. Visual "assets" were analog too. Presentations were drawn on poster board or presented on 35mm slides. Illustrators created imagery with paint or pencils at drafting tables, and film or magnetic tape captured a moving image. The reliance on mail and shipping was significant. The analog world was mechanical and manually driven.

Heavier electronic business transactions and tasks used large and expensive computers. These devices were slow compared to today's standards and transitioned from using vacuum tubes, transistors and punch cards to an integrated microcomputer. Huge, room sized mainframes were installed to handle the transactions with, for most, an unintelligible machine language. On the Information Technology (IT) side, a technician was concerned with managing and maintaining the machine language and the hardware to run it.

As a result, it was quite easy to point out the divide between IT and the ones who depended on IT from business side. The average knowledge worker and IT technician rarely mixed—unless there was a good reason. Mainframes and networked terminal workstations brought in an elite but rudimentary collaboration.

Growing Collaboration

Through the 70's and 80's, machine-based data became more accessible with rudimentary, but more human friendly interfaces and time saving devices. Fax machines became a standard document courier. Noisy dot-matrix printers were popular. Pocket calculators replaced slide rules for many people. LCD screens and personal computers emerged outside of the mainframe. A workplace became more efficient and IT departments were pulled closer toward the business side as technical improvements increased. Although they would seem primitive and crude by today's standards, the new capabilities were highly advanced breakthroughs. With new technologies came new workflows. New challenges had to be overcome, but the networked, electronically collaborative workplace was spreading.

Structured Data

By the late 80's, desktop terminals and personal computer demand skyrocketed, and text and numeric data, once buried within machine language was now accessible to everyday folks on the business side. This "structured data," operated in unprecedented concert with the machine language. A knowledge worker could accelerate work using new electronic tools. This transition from analog survival to a few digital enhancements fostered widespread user adoption and greater efficiencies.

Examples of these improvements were seen wherever typical structured data processes were used instead of paper. Now knowledge workers began to update price lists, sales reports, order administration, and payments by customers much faster.

These were generally predictable, routine tasks that could be entered into structured tables such as to:

Document a Sales Transaction:

Customer	Customer ID	Date of Transaction	Amount	Order #
Mary Smith	#1234	4/20/1987	$100.00	#4567

Manage Accounts Receivable:

Customer ID	Date Due	Balance	Order #
#1234	5/20/1987	$100.00	#4567

Document Negotiated Payback Terms:

Customer ID	Order #	Balance	Terms
#1234	#4567	$100.00	Pays in Pennies

These transactions and documents worked well when dealing with text and numbers within programmed business logic. Data could go into a spreadsheet or a database and used by ancillary systems for understanding trends, faster accounting, and other business affairs. Applications and systems could, with enough understanding of a transactional workflow, be built to support and automate more processes. Even documenting the most heated negotiations or price fluctuations, the data's implied value or meaning might change, but could usually be captured, linked and managed in a structured way.

Today we use structured data in ways that seem magical compared to those early days, but conceptually it is the same. Structured data is able to maintain its structure regardless of its state. It can be stored and protected similar to traditional analog means; instead of paper in file folders cabinets, data began to be stored on floppy drives or tape. As data was entered into transactional applications and systems, information could be searched, retrieved, and moved fluidly through an organization.

The Nature of Structured Data

If you enter numbers or text into a spreadsheet, you have created structured data. Both machines and people can manage this data quite well by sorting the list numerically or alphabetically, editing it, finding and replacing values, importing it into a database and many other actions.

When structured data sets are grouped, combined and compared, companies can do more than review the information, they can derive knowledge. Today many companies warehouse all of its structured data and gain vast insight through this grouping and combining. New industries have emerged offering business analytics and predictive models based on "Big Data." When managed well, the science of structured data analytics wields significant power.

The Internet Disruption

Through the 90's, the attention by both IT and the business side continued primarily on managing structured data. Desktop publishing began to take hold and graphic image files were brought into the equation. This was relatively manageable until 1993 when the popularity of computer based video, on-line bulletin boards and a revolutionary "web browser", primarily invented by a team led by Marc Andreessen, disrupted everything. Now images, graphics and even video required integration with the structured data.

These digital media files consisted of the same rudiments of binary code as text, but the problem was, because they were more "objects" in nature rather than text "strings," this data was considered to be "unstructured."

Unstructured Data

There's a significant difference between structured and unstructured data. Imagine you have another spreadsheet but this time, you want to manage a group of digital photographs. Although you might attempt to paste the photos into cells, these objects can't be structured in the same manner as text or numbers. The images cannot be sorted by color or size, or handle a search for pictures that contain a 'black shirt man' for example. These special files were referred to "rich media." Because they were unique as compared to the form of structured data, they needed special attention. The trouble began when we approached unstructured data management as if it could be managed as structured.

Creative Chaos

Marketing, video production, photo management and other creative knowledge work is less transactional, seldom predictable, more collaborative and iterative. The steps involved to produce a final design doc (a deliverable) include research, production, various approvals, rework, and delivery steps. While the result of a creative process may be in the form of an unstructured digital media photograph, there remains a high dependency on structured data that describes and helps understand it (location, date, and time of a photo-shoot, photographer's name, contract price, and rights).

Other types of digital media oriented knowledge workers, such as product marketers; archivists and librarians needed similar capabilities of linking media files to information. Marketers want to get brand activations to potential customers faster. Librarians and archivists deal with digital media products as well as physical items with related imagery.

While similar to analog in their work steps at a macro level, by the late 1990‘s and into the 2000‘s, the business side demanded greater computerized efficiency and capability. The hope was to manage all aspects of content creation, management, and delivery using structured and unstructured data working in harmony. Success was defined as manipulating and controlling rich digital media as elegantly as text. As a result, media acquisition, management and delivery required radical changes.

Unstructured Data Management

As software and hardware demands expanded, so did the myriad of solutions. New vendors took on the challenge of developing digital content related systems but had to solve the problem of managing unstructured data as if it were structured. This would only be possible through the use of automated workflows and metadata. Metadata, often described as "data about the data," is more accurately defined as "structured data used to describe and manage unstructured data." With this as a foundational concept, new systems, industries, and discipline categories have sprung up to manage the life cycles of media file and metadata management. Some of these generally accepted disciplines include:

ECM

Enterprise Content Management (ECM) is a general, arguably outdated term, for the overall means of organizing and storing an organization's documents, and other content, that relate to the organization's processes. The term encompasses strategies, methods, and tools used throughout the life cycle of the content and related information. Digital asset management, records management and document management are considered by many to be sub-categories of ECM.

CMS/WCM

Content management systems (CMS) are applications that enable iterations within publishing, editing and modifying content, organizing, and other management activities from a central interface. A web content management (WCM) system, a specific form of content management, is a software system that provides website authoring, collaboration, and administration tools designed to allow users with little knowledge of web programming or markup languages to create and manage website content with relative ease.

MOM/MRM

Marketing operations management (MOM) is the strategic alignment of people, process and technology to support marketing activities and improve marketing effectiveness. Marketing resource management (MRM) provides the software infrastructure to support marketing operations management. These terms are also considered by many to be outdated but the concepts remain. Today, many use MarTech, or Marketing Automation to capture this discipline.

LMS

A Learning Management System (LMS) is an application for the administration, documentation, tracking, reporting and delivery of electronic educational technology (also called e-learning) courses or training programs. LMS is a niche of content management.

DAM and MAM/PAM/BAM

Digital asset management (DAM) consists of management tasks and decisions surrounding the ingestion, annotation, cataloguing, storage, retrieval and distribution of digital assets.

Media Asset Management (MAM) systems, a sub-category of DAM, are designed to manage files, typically larger, moving, time based media including animations, videos and music. Generally, MAM systems are designed as a “play-out to air” or an extension of a post production environment.

Production Asset Management (PAM), which is again oriented around film or video assets managed during a film or video production.

Brand asset management (BAM), another sub-category, include computer software and hardware systems that aid in the process of maintaining the consistency of brand assets.

Supporting Infrastructure

In addition to these categories are infrastructure systems and methodologies created to support them. These include enterprise data and cloud architectures, storage with hierarchical storage management and backup, various network protocols, software development frameworks such as Java Script, .NET, and a plethora of user interface options and Application Programming Interfaces (APIs).

When a “Tech Team” Leads DAM Initiatives

Today, well-run IT departments or vendors are vital to any organization. However, unless a given tech team is already proficient in best practices, strategies and technologies to support metadata enabled media workflows, the default reaction might be to focus their solution on storage and access technology. Why does this happen? They handle the inner workings of an organization and concern themselves with many areas:

1. General Electronic Infrastructure
2. Hardware and Availability
3. Operating Systems
4. Networks
5. Storage, Backup, Disaster Recovery, and Data Integrity
6. Data Security and Integrity
7. Access and Permissions
8. Firewalls
9. Spam Filtering and Virus Protection
10. Data Isolation, Routing and Monitoring
11. Users and Electronic Directories
12. User Security and Passwords
13. User Groups and Roles

14. Applications and Databases

15. File Transfer and Inter-Office Connectivity

An tech team usually works within a procurement process with a strong expertise in and attention to the above list. While predictable structured data management fits nicely into traditional IT procurements, technology requirements and storage paradigms, rich media management needs, do not. When a tech team leads a DAM initiative, it has its perspective rooted in something other than DAM. Their approach typically is to solve unstructured rich media management needs with structured data management methodology.

The approach and thinking centers on storage and access technology. This is a world where data, documents as well as rich media, are "just files" and need to be stored, secured and accessed. Executives and teams with no understanding of DAM are often lost in the techno jargon, lose interest, and go down the IT centered path. The stop-gap solution is often to store media files into folders and isolate certain parts of that server into groups to limit access that way. Others may take the same attitude as some tech teams when Mac computers are involved: "Let them deal with it." Some IT teams toss the problems over to Google Drive, iCloud, Drop Box, and any number of other collaborative storage offerings.

Within these solutions, the nuances and demands of a creative process with a dynamic media life cycle is unwittingly missed or misunderstood. As a result, when the business side abdicates DAM analysis and requirements to an IT department, too much is handed over. There will be a strong pull toward the default storage and access approach. One should not automatically assume that if IT is involved in a DAM project, it is doomed to failure. On the contrary, successful projects are achieved only when an IT department or IT project manager and team are active partners. The conflict between the IT side and business side is often a clash between competing digital priorities and perspectives.

When the Business Side Leads the Initiative

When the business side wants to manage media, their focus is on making manual processes faster. They typically lack the knowledge of IT best practices regarding servers, security and technical policies. Of course, a tech team might be "waiting at the gate" with a traditional plan.

When a department from the business side leads a project with minimal IT or DAM expertise, a system is selected primarily by price, user interface, a short list for features that save them time or do something fancy, a reliance on vendor promises, and then hosted on the cloud (sometimes to avoid the IT department entirely). Regardless of which department leads, many forge ahead without the fundamentals covered. The goal is to solve the immediate problems at hand. They have a budget, a list of problems, and thousands of technical options. There is no mature digital strategy to be found. That's not their job. Their job is to get their work done and there's no incentive, nor time to think about such things.

Digital strategy, optimizing workflows, unifying metadata, consolidation or migration, or wider stakeholder requirements are something for somebody else. But there is nobody else in a given organization. The result is, a DAM system, cloud based “file-drop” site, SharePoint or storage systems become viable, albeit misguided options. What most organizations actually look for and buy is a “smart hard drive.” Bypassing a DAM initiative as part of a digital strategy, the effort is minimized to what I call Digital Asset Storage (DAS) rather than Digital Asset Management.

DAS is not DAM

It is not my intention to create yet another term in our already burgeoning acronym alphabet soup, but it’s important to make a distinction between the two paths occurring. You will know your DAM initiative is actually on the “DAS track” when leadership refers to it as an IT problem. The solution is limited to procuring a better way to store digital assets, naming of files and folders, maintaining a folder hierarchy through policy, creating security through heavy administration, reliance on Windows or Mac operating system applications (Windows Explorer, FTP, or Mac Finder) to upload, move and download them, or complex means to deliver the files.

When DAS is the true nature of an initiative, product managers, marketing teams, archivists, and librarians, have, by default, become the media managers themselves, forced to work within a world of folder and file naming conventions. They use their own memory or ask others for help in activities such as search, version control, and file level security.

DAS Digital Asset Storage	DAM Digital Asset Management
Heavy reliance on servers, hard drives, email, and applications	An aligned, unified central platform emerging from strategy
Technology is primary	Business strategy is primary
Department led technology solution	Clearly communicated strategy across the business
Pockets of understanding about the benefits	Executive management and staff alignment and buy-in
Departmentally supported and used	Organizational structures supporting required business units.
Inconsistent naming, long approval cycles, work-arounds	Best practices (Standards, Workflows, and Metadata)
Funded from a department budget	Funded from cross functional, corporately governed budget
Traditions are upheld and territories are protected	Change is managed and communicated effectively
Technology for only a specific asset type and its workflow	Appropriate and scalable technology architecture regardless of asset type or workflow
Make a poor process faster	Build value through an optimized, properly represented, cross functional initiative, enabling digital maturity

In DAS, everyone is praying nobody gets sued for infringing on copyrights. DAS is the storage and access approach. It may be a while before the issues with this approach are realized. Ask anyone who has purchased several solutions over the years but the efforts were in vain. Many resources are activated and wasted in the quest to solve the wrong puzzle.

Let’s solve the right one.

...

2 SOLVING THE RIGHT PUZZLE

The True Goal of DAM

There are tens of thousands of departments and entire companies attempting to solve the DAM puzzle in a myriad of ways. For some, a goal of managing digital assets is limited to loading photographs into a shared desktop folder, while for others, it may require the curating of thousands of video files destined for a commercial website. Whatever one's role within the creation, ingestion, repurposing, archiving, delivery, or monitoring of digital assets, organizations must accept DAM as something different from a typical IT project or application. This is especially true for brands seeking to break out of digital survival, avoid lawsuits, or expand. Rich media is the currency of brand marketing and modern communication. Those that want to deal with the problem are those usually closest to it.

Lacking any kind of legitimate management method, a "champion" will emerge to solve some of the media file problems and attempt to justify a budget. While some hire DAM practitioners or consultants, others don't know what to do and go directly to vendor demos. Others rely on industry analyst reports or buy from familiar, creative tool brand names. Many wait until after a RFP (Request for Proposal) is written, submitted and returned before starting any strategy. Not only does this limit the potential value to the organization, it usually trades best practices for familiar analog methods.

Eventually a system is purchased and deployed. Processes begin to change and a shift in thinking occurs. Users recognize the advantages and opportunities DAM offers, and will want even more efficiency and capability. But a storage array or a small cheap (or even expensive) DAM system seldom scales to their new vision and needs. Over time, users hit a wall of capability, hindering adoption, or they become frustrated by how working with a DAM system takes longer than previous methods.

Ultimately they abandon the system and return to their trusty manual means of media storage, cryptic file naming, and inefficient workarounds. Other departmental champions ri up, shop for yet another system, but this time for themselves. Over time, media storage applications and one-off departmental DAM, CMS and other systems grow like weeds.

If Technology Was the Answer...

When auditing all the technical systems, software applications, and silos in which companies invest to solve DAM-related issues, it's fascinating to step back and ponder at what's there. While some have a beautiful constellation of platforms and user delight, most have a maze. System silos are the usual problem. Some of the systems hold metadata and others only media files, while others might hold both. Often these systems are set up by teams without a knowledge of DAM best practices as outlined above. While a successful technology deployment is a large piece, it's by no means the whole puzzle. Most organizations continue to throw money at more applications and wonder why it isn't making a difference. If technology was the answer, they would have solved it already.

This situation goes on in companies of every size, even ones you'd never suspect, and is the rule rather than the exception. Today, I see solving the wrong puzzle as a real issue. The problem is not selecting the right application or hardware. The problem is not laziness, complacency or lack of interest. The problem is not IT or the business side. The problem is justifying a DAM initiative as a fundamental and required strategy to enable digital maturity.

Digital Maturity

Digital is such an overused buzzword that has virtually lost its meaning. As a result, defining what "digital" means to an organization is required. I often invite DAM managers and teams to explain the term by asking, "What is your Digital Strategy?" Usually the answer centers on social media marketing or a digital product such as a video or e-book. Few in a given company can articulate the digital strategy however.

How an organization operates, how it markets products and services, how it sells them, and even what is sold must emerge from a digital strategy. Markets today consist of different groups and types of people engaged in a digital conversation. However, just as departments default to analog thinking to manage media, companies use outdated analog strategies and attempt to port them to digital outlets. Posting comments on Facebook or Twitter, or offering rich media products for sale is not a digital strategy.

Companies operating within a well defined digital strategy win. Some can sell low value or even mediocre products but maintain a high brand value because of this. These brands have embraced rich media and understand the market conversation, measure and satisfy customer journeys, and how leverage and monetize digital assets.

Market disrupting companies such as AirBnB, Uber, RedBull and others have embraced DAM not only as a means of creating efficiencies, but also to achieve a mission of continuous transformation to higher digital maturity.

A shift to digital maturity is not possible without DAM. When DAM is justified as a software deployment without rationalizing it within a legitimate digital strategy, teams will focus on the pesky file management problem areas mentioned. No system will support the business side's ever increasing demand for a high return on marketing investment nor optimize its creative processes. Nor will they win. With this disconnect in heavy practice today, instead of digital maturity, a business remains mired in digital survival. The demanding digital world is no match for companies entrenched in traditional analog thinking working hard just to keep up.

It's critical then to promote a DAM initiative as a key factor of digital maturity when justifying an investment to a CFO, CIO, and other executives. While digital maturity, strategy and similar concepts may not resonate immediately with executives, it is actually congruent with their objectives as they battle within a chaotic market.

What do executives want?

Beyond the daily concern for sales, investor relations, balance sheet indices, EBITDA calculations and P/E ratios, they are looking for dynamic but manageable growth. When a team brings up the subject of DAM as an application, the message executives' take away is the company needs media file management (DAS). The thinking then follows that file management is all about storage, and servers, and firewalls and all that. The conclusion is to direct it to the CIO's technical team and solve it as an IT issue. Even though DAM is a business strategy, it's neither one that is taught in business school nor particularly highlighted in marketing technology vendor landscapes.

Suppose DAM is advocated within a pharmaceutical company. While media oriented teams call for a central repository and easier search methods, executives are wondering "How will DAM help us sell more medication?" Top executives think in terms of ROI and strategic advantage and justifying DAM is no exception. Therefore, to advocate a DAM initiative to executives based on "file management efficiencies" will only suppress the argument.

There must be a financial return on investment, competitive advantage or another perceived strategic benefit. While executives walk around wanting increased sales and improved shareholder value, DAM champions and teams advocate proportionately minor benefits to them such as process improvement or cost reduction. This disconnect of priorities fails to satisfy executives' needs and is why DAM initiatives end up as IT projects. A fully funded initiative is one that supports the executive's real needs. Therefore, the higher DAM's strategic benefits directly improve the dynamic, manageable growth executives desire, the better the argument.

We'll cover the pieces of the business case in greater detail later, but advocating DAM as the path to a digital maturity will resonate with executives as something more valuable than another software application. This approach serves to align executives, operations and the ever expanding digital conversation with markets.

Tapping into the Digital Conversation

Millennials, also referred to as "digital natives," have never known a world without Internet access to information. The youngest of these are annoyed by screens uncontrollable by touch, pinching and swiping. Most live and work in a seamless digital experience. The more a company understands and services this experience, the more engaged digital natives become. "Digital immigrants," are those who have successfully transitioned from the analog, AM/FM, three television network, paper-based world to an ever accelerating, digitally driven lifestyle and economy. I am a digital immigrant by definition and work with many in my camp as well as many digital natives.

There are also many "digital tourists," who still double click on web links, print out emails and fax back replies, or store all their digital photos and documents on their computer's desktop. These lovely folks are those who cannot, or will not, embrace the digital language and conversation. This is not a criticism, but a reality. Not only are we likely to be related to a few digital tourists, but we may even be one ourselves. We all certainly know a few.

Markets are replete with these types but all engage in a brand's digital conversation in some way. This conversation is so powerful, that companies and their marketing agencies no longer have the final say on a brand's value. Today, the digital conversation is the brand. A company's digital strategy will continually seek to understand, participate and improve within this conversation, or lose to others that do.

For most of us, we enjoy the digital experience when it is, at a minimum, an intuitive experience, or at best, invisible to us. We like companies who fluidly help us get stuff done or engage in a conversation. They meet our expectations, make it easy to do business with them, and understand how we think and how we buy. If I am a digital native, this is a high bar. Digital natives want their brand experience to not only offer a product or service, but enhance their life wherever they may be. Digital immigrants may have to work a little to participate, but will figure it out. If I'm a digital tourist, I'll hope their website helps me find a store nearby, or a way to view their catalog and an 800 number.

We have ample electronic engagement methods with digitally savvy companies when needing hotels, flights, car services, software, food or any kind of shopping. This is not to say that digital engagement is preferred to old fashioned personal attention. It is often, however, a compelling substitute when speed, convenience, or economics are on the line. This is where a digital conversation thrives and digital strategies succeed or fail. Digitally mature companies will align their operations within a well articulated digital strategy. If properly aligned, a brand will dominate a market whether run by natives, tourists or immigrants. A digitally mature company focuses their digital strategy on:

1. Digital Conversation Analytics
2. Continuous Stakeholder On-boarding
3. Refinement
4. Repeat

Digital Conversation Analytics

Markets will react, ignore or respond to marketing activations and conversations, but without an organization measuring or knowing what it all means, it's pointless to invest in them. Many companies have Twitter accounts or Facebook pages, but haven't a clue why or even what they yield. Often a social media channel is used only because it's what everyone else is doing. This is an indication of more digital survival and analog thinking.

Digitally mature companies operate entirely based on data. Data analytics is an important corporate initiative and for good reason. Whether an activation is successful, products or services are sold or a market changes, digitally mature companies understand what's happening. Analytics tells us what the conversation is in a market: the reach, the response, the resulting sentiment, and the lead to revenue cycle. When these data points are understood and managed, executives can devote resources to continuous customer on-boarding.

Continuous Stakeholder On-boarding

Since data explains the conversation, companies will know what is working, what isn't, what to do or make, and where to invest. With these tools and insight, companies not only produce more effective marketing, but can ultimately predict what customers will do and what they will buy next. This process provides opportunities well beyond marketing however.

Well built analytics will indicate and confirm how stakeholders operate. These stakeholders could be customers or investors. Analytics explains how customers buy, when they buy, and even what they buy. Investors, product design, customer service, manufacturing and even engineering should understand this data as it appropriately relates to them. Companies that win, whether in a purely digital market or brick and mortar, align the data with strategic planning, appropriate execution, enhance the conversation, and move stakeholders to join them.

The customer "lead to revenue" journey therefore, rests upon data and the digital engagement an organization extends. Media is the currency of a digital experience, and is often the nature of the conversation itself. User generated content, product and brand deposits and other digital content strengthens the engagement journey. Analytics will however indicate why, what and where assets and content are best used and how DAM should support it. Blasting out content hoping for a sale is a far different growth strategy than aligning media with operations guided by analytics.

What does this look like when it works?

1. Measure the latest operational and marketing baseline data of activities, reach and consumption against sales opportunities, actual sales and customer journeys. DAM protects assets used for brand voice, marketing best practices, product spin and media to be sent as content to publishing channels.
2. Data analysis suggests new products, designs, market preferences and hot spots, as well as customer service refinement opportunities or engineering improvements. DAM supports the efficient control of media assets for product development, customer self-service and new product marketing collateral.
3. Data analysis suggests points within the customer journey where media would be best positioned or dynamically served. DAM pushes media to publishing, product, social and marketing channels, as directed by customer journeys and behavior data.
4. Analytics measures marketing penetration, media consumption against lost or closed sales at key points during the customer journey. DAM maintains rights of demanded media as well as correct versions, language, and format.
5. Data unmasks emerging gaps or opportunities in the customer journey as sales and media consumption are compared to operational and marketing baselines. Work orders to create more effective assets are created, and DAM supports

the overall media supply chain from creation to measurement.

6. Return to step 1.

Organizations that use DAS will never get anywhere near this level of automation or power. Instead of a digitally mature platform, they are mired in "digital survival." We've considered many examples of the causes and effects of mismanaged media, but including a lack of analytics to the equation will only continue the spiral downward.

Companies in digital survival mode will spend more on technology, hire more people, and chase unwieldy strategies. The ever-spinning effort looks productive because there is a lot of activity and purchasing of tools to stop the digital bleeding, but will be moot when competing with digitally mature companies.

The process of moving from digital survival to maturity is called digital "transformation." Digital transformation is discussed in many white papers and conference topics. However, digital transformation implies a never-ending journey without a goal. A goal of digital maturity will unlock a renewed vision for an organization and create a laser focus on what a DAM initiative offers. Without DAM, they'll never make it and wonder why all the technology with project overload and new hires aren't making a difference.

When executives, like any other team with budget, start their digital strategy with buying a system or solving marketing technology problems, they will succeed only if they are very experienced with current DAM practices and technologies. In my experience, executives who approve applications to handle DAM needs without a foundational digital maturity strategy will find their luck quickly running out. No matter how many re-orgs are done, the issues won't improve.

DAM should be, to executives, more than file management for a tech team to solve; it should be a primary component, in tandem with analytics, of a mature digital strategy. This approach is more compelling and accurate depiction of DAM's value and potential benefit to this stakeholder group. When one is creating a business case for DAM, this vision should be at the heart of it.

...

"Who the heck enters all the metadata?"
- Marketing Manager

3 TURNING THE PIECES OVER

What is DAM?

Though it uses databases, DAM isn't a database. It uses software, but doesn't work by installing an application. It leverages processes, workflows, and file management policies, but it's not merely an archive or process engine. It handles unstructured data through metadata, but it's more than that. It can affect and can be affected by a company's creative, legal, marketing, operations, IT and sales needs, preferences and policies. DAM isn't technology or a smart hard drive or a tool to fix media chaos. It isn't any one piece of the puzzle. DAM is a business strategy fundamental to companies of any size or market. It's a primary, often forgotten component of a mature enterprise content management strategy.

I sometimes get a call after a system is installed and something is wrong. Executives aren't getting the return on a technical investment they already made and departments are looking for another system, people aren't using it, or vendors didn't disclose major limitations. Optimally, I'll be invited to help an organization prior to a purchase and develop a business case that includes a strategic roadmap, a technical plan, total cost of ownership over a period of years, and specific best operational practices. I'll conduct workshops to develop metadata, workflows or plan for consolidating many repositories into one. The goal is to develop a strategy.

Waiting until after an RFP is sent and returned is not the time to develop a DAM strategy. A hard drive, cloud site or publishing to Facebook is not a strategy.

A minimal amount of education is required just to get everyone using a common vocabulary and philosophy about what DAM should do...and what it should not do. Usually after a short assessment, I can visualize the operational, management and technical platform an organization requires. My goal is to build acceptance of a DAM initiative, not merely a system. While this is somewhat esoteric, ultimate success will be achieved when DAM is invisible to an organization and the business is thriving in digital maturity.

When someone asks what I do for a living, I'm tempted to say I help people with their DAM problems or that I'm a DAM consultant. I spend my days in DAM meetings. The jokes get old, and are endless. Clearly, as an industry, Digital Asset Management doesn't have the best acronym. But sometimes it works to break the ice. Such as when I'd ask, "What's your DAM problem?" Posing this question usually worked pretty well, until it came off a bit harsh with a group of sweet ladies in a church.

Today I ask, "What's your DAM puzzle?" It's a simple question, but the answer can be complex. What I mean by it is, "How does your organization manage its digital assets? What do you think could be better? What would you like to solve?"If your company works with photos, graphic files, presentations, marketing collateral, advertising or video, your company is trying to manage its digital assets. The processes and systems used to handle them, however, may be adding to the confusing conundrum. Unsolved DAM puzzles can be expensive, limit a business' innovation and creativity and growth. What's your DAM puzzle? There are many areas that show us the evidence. Once you begin to look, you'll start to see things differently.

Start by looking for media files scattered across shared network folders, portable drives and an excessive reliance on email. Consider a major advertising agency I know that had stored digital assets in shared folders for many years. All of its images, video clips, InDesign files, creative briefs, and job information were stored, accessed, and shared within the myriad of folders. Everyone in the agency was trained on how to set up a folder hierarchy for a new project according to some complex process of nesting folders and naming them correctly. Eventually everyone got the idea that this was where one went to find stuff.

Each staff member had to navigate through an elaborate folder maze every day. Files were moved around from one folder to the next depending on what was happening to that project. A video file would be named Soap Commercial v1.Mov, then a new version, Soap Commercial v2.Mov, would appear (then New Commercial V 3 Final.Mov, then New Commercial V3 Final Real FINALApproved.Mov) and so on.

If a file was named incorrectly, moved to another location, or got deleted, the whole process was halted and it became a catastrophe. When a file couldn't be found, staff made calls to coworkers, then called outside suppliers, and then emails started flying. In this client situation, I calculated an average number of project related emails sent that concerned looking for digital assets, reviewing work, updating status, and delivering the content. The average was 918 emails. (This was per project!) Which, essentially, is a lot of wasted time sending emails back and forth.

Another factor was the number of shared folders needed to manage the digital assets of all 12 of their brands. My audit revealed that they had over 530,000 folders. That's a large volume, to be sure, but the real DAM puzzle was what those folders contained and what their effect was. Those folders contained over 17 million job files. Twenty-eight percent were duplicates, despite the de-duplication technologies deployed. These folders consumed 180 terabytes of data. That's enough to store the Library of Congress several times over. There were a lot of places to look for any one file.

Consider the wasted internal staff and/or outsourced agency time your own company spends on just looking for digital assets when they are locked up somewhere among thousands of folders. How much more time is spent looking for approval or rights status, reformatting, transcoding, and delivering digital assets? Many agencies like this one got the DAM message and are now running far better than before. The folder, hard drive, and email approach can be solved, even if it's been relied on for many years.

Another example comes from the marketing department in a company of about 1000 people. This particular company sold a variety of products and used images in their company website, print material, catalogues, advertising, and use for customer support. We calculated that each image costs, on average, $127 to create.

Though it was a small firm, other departments, such as support, engineering, and legal, all had their own budgets for creating and storing digital assets. The result was that each department was constantly looking in other departments, again in shared folders and desktops, for an image. When it couldn't be found, it was created over again. More time and dollars wasted. Sometimes this scavenger hunt for the right image was just too time-consuming, and staff would order more images from their photographer or agency. Sometimes the photograph was retaken with a digital camera or even an iPhone. Some were grabbed off of Google Images.

In another example, which was by no means unusual, a marketing manager wanted an image he had seen of a potential product. It took many people over a week to find the photo. In the end, it wasn't even used. If I were the Chief Marketing Officer, I'd want my marketing teams to stay creative and innovative, keeping my product marketing and brands fresh, rather than wasting their time searching for something. As this goes on all the time in many organizations, some people could more accurately update their job title to "Media Scavenger."

Another way to find evidence of a DAM puzzle is to count how many individual systems your company uses to manage digital assets. Beyond the shared folders, you might have photo management databases, partner websites, product information databases, individual desktops, SharePoint, or shelves, binders and boxes of tapes, portable drives, photographs, and discs. A major corporation has thousands of partners, staff and suppliers. This company has one brand to manage and is a top advertiser and brand marketer. Now, one would think that to manage one brand across the globe, a single digital asset repository would be enough.

Yet, in my research, I uncovered nearly 50 separate digital asset repositories. Each of them required IT staff time, upgrades and maintenance, user management, bandwidth, and backup. But there were even more troubling operational issues. Anyone who wanted to find anything often had to be trained on another system. There was no single naming convention or folder schema. One system would call a file the ASSET ID, while another just called it "NAME." The systems didn't generally talk to each other, and if something moved from one to another, information had to be entered again. In the event that one system pushed information through some kind of connector or web service, routine maintenance or upgrades would force that portion of the system down for hours or even several days. With dozens of systems to manage and maintain, portions of the system were frequently down.

As a result, with so many systems up one day then down the next, few trusted them. Then the real puzzle emerged. Staff members hoard their digital assets on their own desktops, servers and hard drives, creating even more disconnected repositories of digital assets. Eventually, the company had dozens of systems that were abandoned or only used if absolutely necessary. The growing silos of digital asset storage led to hidden costs. Think about the redundant amount of file backup going on every night, increasing network and storage loads. Each year the company in this example would spend hundreds of thousands of dollars on storage just to keep up with the demands.

Luckily for this company, they are now on a single DAM system and are extending it across the enterprise.

Looking for media files scattered across shared network folders, portable drives, and an excessive reliance on email is only one piece of the puzzle you may discover. Another area to review is how well you, your staff, and your legal counsel know which videos, music, and photographs can be used for what purpose, in which location and for how long. How is this information communicated? I have found that telephone or emails are the main means. How often is someone interrupted to ask about a particular asset's clearance? I have to ask, are you the person they call?

Having marketing collateral, for example, with insufficient or no usage rights information can bankrupt a company. One of the most classic missteps in poor rights management I know of comes from a large manufacturer of consumer electronics. You've definitely seen their ads and you probably own something they make—or at least you want something they make. They are extremely smart and innovative. Yet, for as clever as they are in creating and marketing their products, they had all of their photos in what they thought was a global digital asset management system. They had tens of thousands of photos that could be searched and retrieved by their internal staff and partners. Instead of locking all their photos in a shared server requiring hours of hunting for photos, they decided that using descriptive metadata would be helpful. And it was.

Marketing teams all over the world used this search capability to find and retrieve their photos for promotions and advertising. However, one photo in particular was accidentally used in Europe for two years on a very successful and popular campaign. The problem was that this photo was licensed for use only in the United States. The photographer discovered the mistake and sued the company. To date, the photographer has won several judgments totaling over $15 million just because of a big “OOPS!” that could have been prevented.

While photos could be searched and accessed, the usage rights were missing. It would take a major overhaul of their digital asset management processes to get things right. Thankfully for them, they did what it took to avoid this in the future. Several companies have gone from paying millions of dollars annually in rights infringement fines to $0.

Clearly DAM can improve efficiency, but the results are realized in strategic benefits. Another issue appears when an organization is oblivious to the opportunities to repurpose assets for increased revenue. A company I know had licensed their logos and images to partners. These logos would be put on hats, beach towels, jackets, and toys. For years, the company sent out a printed catalog for logos and approved images at a substantial cost. Eventually the company deployed a web portal with a back end digital asset management system.

Designers developed logos and other imagery while

"cybrarians" managed the DAM system. Everything was connected, from acquisition to management and editorial, through review and approval and then, finally, to delivery. By using a web portal as a distribution channel, all of the images and logos were available to the right license partner and delivered in the right format. This improved their licensing cycle time by over 80% and increased their revenue five times over the next two years.

Finally, many organizations deploy marketing automation systems, web content management, e-Commerce, product life cycle management, collaboration, and content translation. Each of these systems handles asset storage and access within their own on-board repository. Without a central, "single source of truth" for all imagery and video, silos are built to support each platform, usually without regard for another.

An enterprise DAM system should handle this, but most organizations as we've seen, don't think this way due to the traditional tech team focus, are limited by its own silo'd departmental budget or political standing. Assets are converted into content ready derivatives and then manually moved and stored across the various repositories. The manual efforts result in wasted time, which grind down the efficiency and increase labor costs. Many corporations are recognizing this and looking to making a change. But will they?

In most of these cases, it's clear that organizations believed that multiple repositories were the answer or that DAM practices were not relevant. Consider how your company spends its time, enables its staff, and invests to manage digital assets for the right business purpose. There are several other areas to review as well. In later chapters, I'll look at how these examples can be used to build a business case. I hope you'll agree that it's time to turn your DAM puzzle into an opportunity that can be solved.

Now that the box is open and turned the pieces over, let's look at what we have.

...

"They have 167 brands and 1 DAM system.
We have 1 brand and 47 DAM systems."
-- Major brand DAM Manager

4 THE MAIN PUZZLE PIECES

The Main Puzzle

What is unique about digital asset management compared to other strategies? How do successful DAM initiatives get started and maintain success? In general, successful DAM initiatives:

1. Are a fundamental component of the organizational digital strategy (not a digital product, channel, or solution).
2. Determine the DAM and digital strategy before sending

RFPs.

3. Support the management during the creation of new assets.
4. Coordinate the ingest of acquired media.
5. Provide secured search and access.
6. Promote reuse and repurpose.
7. Deliver original or derivative content to publishing systems.
8. Leverage and/or manage optimized workflows.
9. Use DAM specific technologies.
10. Attract and delight stakeholders with any technology.
11. Control the creation or expansion of needless silos.
12. Have proper oversight by the right teams.
13. Promote the business side to lead the DAM initiative.
14. Include the IT side as a partner (unless the IT department has a DAM practitioner leading).
15. Communicate and adhere to best practices.
16. Justify the initial and ongoing funding, technology, staffing and strategy.

These critical factors must be maintained by DAM teams. Successful initiative teams do not shop for a system as an initial step. Shopping without planning will set the course for exploding system silos, worker confusion, higher costs, profit erosion and productivity loss. Justified technology vendor engagements must come later.

Successful initiative teams also pay careful attention to any motion to call vendors for pricing, or to use non-DAM systems as viable alternatives. Typical IT departments, recognizing a need to improve workflows, file access and storage practices, will steer their attention to a non-DAM or DAS approach. This occurs when DAM practices are misunderstood or disregarded. DAM teams who know better will properly handle these actions. Teams that struggle with knowing which direction to go are usually confused at a fundamental level. A good place to start is understanding the difference between an "asset" and "content."

The Nature of an Asset

What exactly is a digital asset and how is it distinguished from other files? Why aren't digital assets referred to merely as media or media files? Is it helpful or more confusing to use the terms "digital asset" and "content" interchangeably? Years ago I saw a compelling demonstration by Michael Moon, one of the pioneers of DAM. He announced that hidden in each of his hands was a piece of paper. In his left hand, he held a paper that would give him $1 off any coffee drink at Starbucks. It was a, however, a paper with special properties.

One property was it could only be redeemed for a coffee drink at Starbucks. Another one was it had to be used prior to an expiration date. Finally, he said, the real special property came immediately after it was handed over to a barista and scanned at the Starbucks checkout counter. At that point, it was worthless. He held up the paper for us to see and, of course, it was a Starbucks coupon. It had a Starbucks logo on it, lots of text outlining terms and conditions, and an expiration date. He said that although the coupon was in his possession, he didn't really own it. Starbucks was the owner and had given him, the redeemer, a limited license to use it.

In his other hand, he said, was another piece of paper which, funny enough, also was worth $1 for a coffee at Starbucks. But this one didn't have a Starbucks logo on it, nor did it have an expiration date. As he held it up, we saw it was a $1 bill. The differences between the two pieces of paper were somewhat obvious, one being a coupon and another legal tender; but he then explained something previously unclear to me.

The coupon, due to its time sensitivity, conditional use and having a license for use, was an example of "content." The dollar bill, having no time sensitivity, conditional use, and it could be owned, was an "asset." It always retains an inherent value of $1 and has no expiration date. If it's given to someone else, that person owns it and can use it as any other asset. What does an asset contain?

Assets have an Essence

The paper used for the dollar bill is the medium of the $1 value. Although the paper is really worthless paper, it's what we use to hold the idea, proxy and transferability of the value. The idea of what that paper represents is considered the "essence of $1." It's what we value. Broken down into actual components, digital assets, while also having a medium such as a .MOV file, the entity or idea of the asset is considered the essence.

The essence of "The Fast and the Furious" is the notion of a movie, not only what is in the file you download or watch at a theater. If you lose your DVD of the movie on a train, you only lose a $1 disc with the essence on it. You haven't actually lost "The Fast and the Furious" as if it were a Ming Dynasty vase.

Assets have Security

If someone steals your Starbucks coupon, you might feel annoyed. If someone takes your $1 bill without asking, you'll feel something completely different. We protect our assets with security such as a bank account, safe deposit box, guard dog, legal documents, anti-counterfeit markings or a wallet.

Digital assets have security too. Some assets should be seen by everyone, others that should be seen only by legal, and others that can be downloaded by marketing. Security policies DAM systems provide very granular security measures while regular file folders do not.

Assets have Metadata

A dollar bill has certain information that indicates that it's legitimate money, and legal tender for all public and private debts. It uses ONE DOLLAR as a mark of its value and a letter code showing where it was made. Digital assets also have information that is used to describe and control it.

Metadata is a fundamental component and is used to describe, control, maintain structure, or understand the content to which it is affiliated. As mentioned earlier, metadata is essentially "structured data used to describe and manage unstructured data." Without it, media supply chains suffer in every conceivable way including extended cycle times, excessive search times, compromised security, and even decreased creative expression.

Although metadata may seem a foreign concept, we actually use it everyday. To understand what metadata is, how it is different from the essence, and its intrinsic value, consider a simple metaphor:

When shopping for a favorite soup at a grocery store, what is valued and desired by the consumer, beyond fulfilling any brand loyalty, is not the metal can or the label, but the soup itself. We consider the bits of information on the can's label as the metadata for the soup.

Thinking of this concept in terms of structured and unstructured data, the information on the label can be copied into a spreadsheet, compared with data, or input into other systems. The soup itself obviously cannot be used in these ways or it would be a mess. The only three methods of understanding the soup is to:

1. Have sufficient information on the label (Good metadata)
2. Open the can and taste it (Downloading and opening)
3. Ask someone who may know about the soup. (Wasting time)

The soup (the essence) is what we really want, but the label (the information about the soup) is used to help identify pertinent details about the soup such as the ingredients, the price/UPC code, the weight, the nutritional value, and when it will expire.

If every soup can had its label removed and shoppers were only able to browse rows of tin cans hoping for the right type, the result would be mass confusion and few cans would be sold. Shoppers would realize that the only way to choose the right soup, is to hope a store worker would remember what

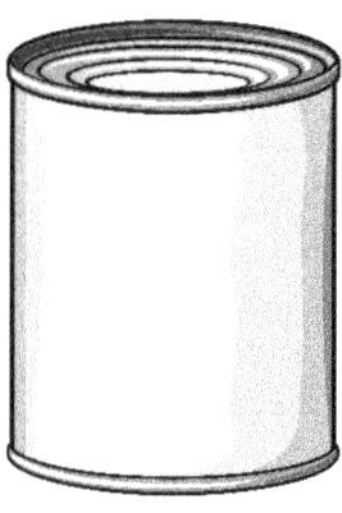

was in the can, or be forced to open the can and try to decipher its contents.

Quality labeling produces confidence in a product. Soup cans with strong branding and labeling cost more than generically labeled cans, even if the contents are exactly the same. We pay higher prices for quality labeling. Our assets, likewise, increase in value with quality metadata.

When considering the metadata for a digital asset, maintaining consistency is critical. Otherwise the file, like the soup, must be "opened" to know what it is. Just as keeping labels for soup cans is critical to maintaining a quality standard, so is maintaining metadata for content files for optimizing its use and control.

With metadata as our asset's label, we can think of it as the information that should travel with the asset. DAM systems connect the asset's media (containing the essence) with the information about it. The better our information, the fewer questions we have about it, the easier it is to find, and the higher the asset's value.

Embedding Metadata in the Asset

A video may have a "director" named John Smith, but a video file doesn't carry around this custom value. The value must be referenced to the linked asset by using a DAM system. Standards such as XMP or IPTC allow metadata to be embedded in the header of the media file. This can be read and written to by better DAM Systems.

One could argue the director's name could be used in the naming of the file or placed in a Directors Folder to maintain this information. But this is a shortsighted workaround that users often adopt. The issue with this is most media files have multiple attributes and would require many names and folder locations. A best practice for DAM is to hold only one version of any asset at anytime. Saving files in folders would require multiple copies.

Some metadata can be carried by the asset itself and be read by systems or applications. Examples of this type of metadata would be the technical metadata, such as an asset's file size or creation date. Other metadata attributed to an asset, depending on the file type and the system used to manage it, can only be linked to the asset and stored in a database.

Metadata Standards

A metadata standard is a schema created by industry groups to provide support for the asset types or workflows it manages within an application. Other systems allow for complete independent and customizable schemas. Better DAM systems use a mixture of both standardized and customizable schemas. It would not be sufficient to use Dublin Core, a popular schema, as the only metadata in a DAM System.

Photography and most creative documents such as graphics, layouts and print materials can use embedded metadata schema models. The metadata within these types of files use standard schemas such as EXIF, IPTC, or XMP. These metadata values are either embedded into the file (information that should not be changed) or might allow a user to create, edit or remove the values that are carried (such as a description or caption).

As long as a file is viewed or edited within a system or application that supports the embedded schema, the metadata will be maintained, indexed by the system and available to authorized users. Video files have typically been more reliant on proprietary file types, applications, and wrappers (such as MXF) to maintain some limited embedded metadata. There are standards that have attempted to expand this video metadata carriage such as IMF.

Designing your Metadata Schema

A good place to begin designing metadata schemas is to analyze and gain consensus on:

1. Your own organization's vocabulary and preferred terms.
2. The required asset types such as video or image formats
3. The appropriate number and types of fields for each type
4. The number of required fields users will need and accept
5. How metadata can be linked or embedded
6. How searches will use the metadata

Metadata Types

In general, metadata schemas can be grouped into four primary categories: Descriptive, Technical, Administrative and Structural.

Descriptive Metadata

This category is information that is used, as expected, to describe the asset. A video clip of a particular woman riding a certain motorcycle on a highway would need a good description for it to be found via search: "A blonde woman rides her blue motorcycle on the 405 near Mulholland Drive". Other metadata of this type include keywords (motorcycle, woman, blonde, blue, highway, California, 405, mountains, Mulholland Drive). Other descriptive metadata would include fields such as Title, Subject, Project ID, etc. These fields are typically used in search and retrieval.

Keywords are an often over emphasized means to describe assets but are better than nothing. But over time, many variant keywords are created without order, consistency or structure, and can create greater difficulty in searches and control. The alternative is to attempt to create too much order and structure using a list of available, selectable terms. This will impede the user experience. The trick is to balance the number of metadata fields, either required or optional, the way users select them and providing freedom within an overall framework of intuitive options.

Technical Metadata

This metadata category provides information about an asset that is typically not editable. These are embedded aspects about the asset such as the bit-rate, file extension/mime type, resolution, aspect ratio, etc. These are useful when determining the proper format for a specific use in repurposing the asset or distribution.

Administrative Metadata

This category deals with the control and use of an asset through out its life cycle. Administrative is divided into two schemas of Rights and Preservation (or Archival).

Rights:

Rights Metadata such as the asset's owner, expiration date, contract ID, are important fields to limit an asset's use. This is different than security. Think of security as limiting what a user can view or do with an asset within a DAM system, whereas rights limits what a user can do with an asset once they have it.

The owner of a large bundle of $1 bills may loan them to someone and charge for the use. Digital asset owners extend rights through a permission or a license for others, for free or by paying a fee, to use it. Even if it's converted into smaller versions, an asset's rights are to be maintained when published into content.

Archival:

Preservation (Archival)

This metadata is used for an asset's long-term preservation and maintenance. An asset will have an indefinite life cycle that may be highly relevant and important to its stakeholders when it is created. Over time, this relevancy may wane but its importance may ebb and flow depending on circumstances. A valued asset may need to be saved in a particular format to preserve it on an archival medium. Over the years, it may need to be "re-preserved" onto another format in certain intervals. Archival metadata informs custodians of assets how to maintain the asset throughout its life cycle.

Structural Metadata

This is used to indicate an asset's placement within other, more complex objects such as a book, layout, or visual effect. An example is a graphic layer being placed behind another layer. The metadata in this case exists to orient one asset in relation to another.

Structural

The Asset

An asset is an amalgamation of all of these components. An asset is the essence and security, linked to structured, predictable,

business oriented metadata. Content therefore, is a derivative of an asset. It is an amalgamation of some of the components of the asset including the essence converted into a publish ready format, rights and license, and channel specific metadata.

Unifying Metadata

Strategically, to reduce the number of silos of automation and disconnected information, DAM managers and teams develop an over-arching master metadata schema to which all systems and users can adhere. Subsets of this overall structure are then used within the various applications and platforms for consistent vocabularies and information data sources. Whether internally or externally exchanged, metadata should use a common schema wherever possible to allow straightforward data mapping between systems. A common mistake is for each department to create its own schema. Over time, this becomes another departmental silo and integration is difficult and costly.

For larger enterprise metadata schemas, (such as Time Warner's metadata structure--masterfully curated by Ms. Abbe Wiesenthal), there are significant challenges with this approach. The best efforts to align every asset under single unified terms can be a long and troubling puzzle. The goal should be to unify metadata sufficiently to ensure seamless processes and predictability across the enterprise, while unifying more thoroughly within a corporate segment.

Metadata Standards

Often organizations will turn to metadata standards such as PRISM, Dublin Core, or for standard image licensing, Plus Coalition. These standards are well suited for certain assets, workflows and industries, but don't offer, nor are intended to offer a complete organizational metadata model. An organization can find these helpful for integration and to conform to industry standards, but are typically incomplete. Standards making bodies, such as SMPTE, or vendors themselves, such as Adobe, Avid, Sony or Apple, attempt to create open standards or frameworks (OMF, IMF, XMP, MXF, QuickTime, AAF, etc.) to aid integration of metadata and published content files.

Even systems that accept the same content files and embedded metadata can require more advanced integration. With no standardized schema mentioned to satisfy every business operation or production pipeline, metadata will often require import-mapping procedures. Mapping is required when one system employing a variety of metadata fields and values, sends those values with another system with similar or entirely different metadata fields. This can occur between departments or separate companies looking to share metadata when a unified schema is not possible.

For example, Company A refers to production work a "job" and Company B considers it a "project" yet each need to share the information. Both job and project mean the same general thing, “work” to each respective company. If Company A sends “job” metadata records to Company B using the original field names, the receiving company will fail to import the values into their system. The receiving company’s system expects to find “projects”, but received “jobs” instead.

To solve this problem, similar or even disparate systems supporting web services such as XML (Extensible Markup Language) or APIs (Application Programming Interfaces), can connect, translate and share metadata.

When Company A sends “job” information to Company B, the metadata is sent as an XML document and a script translates that information to “project” fields to ensure compatibility with Company B’s system. It imports without an issue if the programming is solid. One misplaced letter and the whole thing will most likely fail.

XML is an open standard text document that is used to transport and store data such as metadata, customer lists, or any other information. XML is readable by both machines and a moderately trained person and provides a powerful means of metadata sharing. Companies needing XML as a metadata sharing process must adhere to strict rules on formatting, naming, case sensitivity, and import/export configuration rules within the system receiving the metadata.

In larger organizations where several platforms or data

repositories are maintained, comprehensive metadata management systems are deployed. Metadata management systems allow users to capture and manage the standard business terminology and structures including vocabularies, preferred terms and object relationships across all disconnected repositories and maintain a common platform.

Users may then search and retrieve results from all metadata repositories for maximum visibility without customized integration through XML. This is particularly useful when searching media assets across completely different business units such as news archives, photo libraries, and marketing collateral.

Organizations that may create integrations of structured data sets into DAM systems should avoid departmental metadata fields or endure significant customizations. This is accomplished by standardizing on metadata conventions wherever possible out of business-oriented strategies. Once the business needs are clear, theses strategies dictate technical requirements rather than technical defaults dictating the business needs.

To understand and optimize processes for managing and controlling assets within a media supply chain, quality metadata (technical, rights, etc.) will be required. Typically, stakeholders of a process are the best sources for metadata fields and their knowledge of the relationships to the assets. Business managers, subject matter experts, and digital workflow specialists can work together to develop schemas out of primary workflows, digital asset types and asset life cycles.

Metadata Quality

The quality of an asset is significantly impacted by how well it is cultivated, curated and maintained throughout its life cycle. It is not uncommon for departments or organizations to start entering metadata for an asset after it is completed or to be entered by users with no real understanding of an asset's value or relevancy. This will yield extremely limited and low value metadata. To improve the quality of metadata, it's important to begin entry of it as early in it's life cycle as possible.

Camera manufacturers provide for geo-location coordinates and other information to be used later other production phases. As specific authorized users of asset elements or various versions of a final asset are developed, small amounts of metadata can be input. Over the course of the production and its release, metadata is refined, cleaned, and updated resulting in a high degree of reliability. Low reliability in metadata will lower trust in systems.

Metadata ownership is a key best practice to maintaining the quality. Organizations that maintain their metadata quality have implemented ownership teams or joint cross-functional accountabilities. Without these in place, departments and organizations will lack confidence in the metadata and overall process.

Business managers within organizations and departments should work closely with their technical managers to create platforms upon which metadata frameworks will be adopted, relied, and scaled. Without these fundamental principles of metadata, assets will be lost, uncontrolled and wreak havoc on already pressured life cycles.

With a clear understanding of the nature and importance of metadata within a media supply chain; the relationship of a DAM system to other related systems can be outlined. This understanding should also prevent the implementation or use of non-DAM systems as a short term solution.

Non-DAM Systems

What is meant by a "non-DAM system?" It is important to understand the differences of the various DAM and non-DAM vendor offerings. Many popular systems deployed to solve DAM puzzles, outside of the ubiquitous file server and hard drive, are not really DAMs, but actually web content systems, orchestrate workflow, or are really archival or built for marketing campaigns, content publishing or distribution, or project management. The need for what these systems offer is certainly real, but using them to handle DAM as well is problematic.

Within any DAM, content management or otherwise, a core "DNA of function" should be identified. The point here is every system will offer some appealing functionality to handle a segment of media management. The larger the segment the system will manage will increase its appeal. The trick is to understand where DAM fits in an overall media supply chain, and where others do and why. Without this knowledge, non-DAM systems will be attractive but ultimately unsatisfactory.

Whether in the operations of product marketing or feature films, the creative artist, executive, manager, or financial team member, professional in a respective field but lacking DAM experience, won't be able to distinguish between these approaches. In many cases, a platform is purchased because it "manages media" in the aggregate sense. As a result, inappropriate technologies or inferior practices are brought in to solve DAM issues.

The Approach Points to the Tool

To illustrate this more, we know of office suites that offer a spreadsheet, word processing, and presentation application. While a presentation may contain text, images, and handle the inclusion of a spreadsheet like table within a slide deck, the idea of using a presentation program for a business letter would be ridiculous. Yet in many cases, the same approach is used within misguided initiatives.

While these examples may seem extreme, an initiative may turn to more general enterprise collaboration solutions such as SharePoint. While this application has user access controls, file sharing, document versioning and can distribute information and assets; in its purest form it is not a viable DAM system. The core DNA of function of SharePoint is project communication and document control, team collaboration management, and content distribution through a web browser.

Another example of a non-DAM system is a storage archive system working in tandem with a shared server folder hierarchy. The idea here is to use software to keep the unwieldy files on a hard drive managed or even offer some search capability. However, some compound documents such as InDesign or certain video file structures must be maintained as a cohesive unit or they will break within these solutions.

While the storage footprint may be improved, the strategy is fundamentally the same as maintaining folders and naming conventions, even with some ability to manage versions or reduce duplication of some files. The core DNA is file storage management, not improving easy "find ability" or DAM related actions.

What is more common, teams will deploy enterprise class WCM, CMS, and Marketing applications that include a file repository and some metadata for users to leverage as its DAM. As the core DNA is helping manage the content publishing segment, any DAM-like function is focused on supporting the file storage needs for this silo. These applications' DAM is built for the WCM specifically. Other systems outside of this silo will need other repositories or a complex web of requests will have to be developed. Upgrading these systems can be an expensive chore.

CMS as a DAM System

Another issue of using a content management system to handle all aspects of a media storage, management, delivery, publishing, project management, and measurement needs is like the popular "all in one" stereo systems of many years ago. This device offered a LP record player, AM/FM radio, 8 track or cassette tape deck, and speakers. While having all of these desired playback devices rolled up into a single box, one traded convenience for performance and quality. The packaged components were either of dubious quality or if of a higher quality, these units were excessively expensive. When the LP record player component broke, it required either a repair or the replacement of the whole stereo. When CDs replaced LPs, to maintain the same functional experience, a serious customization was required or the owner went shopping for a new system. While a working stereo with its bundled components would work for personal listening, it would not be usable within, for example, a legitimate radio station.

Today with our smart phones and the associated app marketplace, we have far greater control over our devices to match our needs and preferences. We may have a single "unit" in the form of a phone or tablet to manage our modules, but we control the functionality and level of quality within that device. We can easily add, delete, replace and upgrade them as needed or desired.

Bundled DAMs within a CMS, WCM or marketing campaign management system produce challenges and limitations similar to the old stereo. Years ago, prior to iPhones or other smart devices, users where offered a few, limited or built in applications. The devices were not designed to be flexible or open to improvement. As organizations need something different or evolve based on growing needs, major customizations or a completely different system to manage media is required in much the same way. How can we develop a unifying strategy to avoid this trap? We need to understand what's really happening.

Supply Chain Management

A standard strategy companies use to maximize return on investment is supply chain management. There are many reasons for this but it allows a retailer for example to reduce their inventory to only what's needed at a given time, remove wasteful rework and errors, and continually improve it to maximize profit. Supply chain management gives us an idea of what is happening within a company as they develop products. The goal is to continuously refine a process to ensure as much return on investment as possible, remove waste or costly work-arounds, and prepare for unexpected factors. Creating efficiencies or strategic benefits in the chain, such as sourcing lower cost manufacturing or consolidating shipments, offers a greater potential for higher profits. Waste, errors and deviations from the expected chain are all enemies of supply chain management. Supply chain managers are on constant alert for any bottlenecks within or costly threats to the chain.

Rework within a manufacturing process is considered costly waste and requires immediate fixes. Delayed shipments that require re-ordering of products are also costly waste. Large amounts of costly waste will justify the hiring of Six Sigma consultants to investigate and suggest improvements. Good managers rely on extremely granular metrics of deliveries, productivity, and deviations. There are supply chain managers

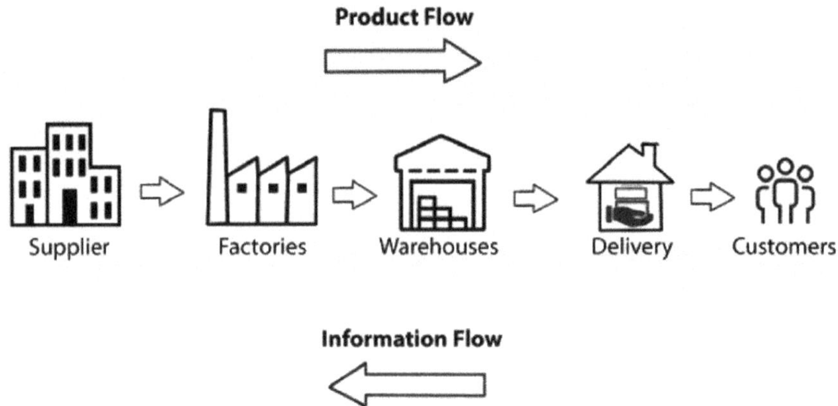

who possess a keen, obsessive scrutiny of key performance indicators within a given supply chain. One in particular can calculate how a problem in a supply chain will affect a product's profitability to within a fraction of a percentage point and in what region.

An analysis can also be done on information chains within business systems. As business information as well as goods flow between suppliers and buyers, or within a company's inter-departmental chain, wasted steps, rework, and inefficiency results in time lags and higher costs. These pop out on daily reports and should generate strong course corrections by managers within well-run companies.

DAM is Media Supply Chain Management

Using supply chain management or business information

exchanges as models, successful DAM initiatives have a clear understanding of its "media supply chain." Instead of raw material working its way across the globe to it's hanging on a retailer's clothes rack, media goes through its own predictable process to be delivered. First is the production and/or acquisition of the media. That media is uploaded or ingested into something (often a hard drive, server or DAM system). The media is managed, that is, named, tagged, searched for, collected, edited, secured appropriately, retouched and/or prepared for preservation or publishing. The prepared media is then converted or transcoded, tagged again, secured appropriately with use restrictions or rights, and delivered to its final storage location or publishing destination. Media activities at each stage are audited for file counts, usage, search methods, security conflicts and many other metrics.

The life cycle of create (or acquisition), ingest, manage, deliver

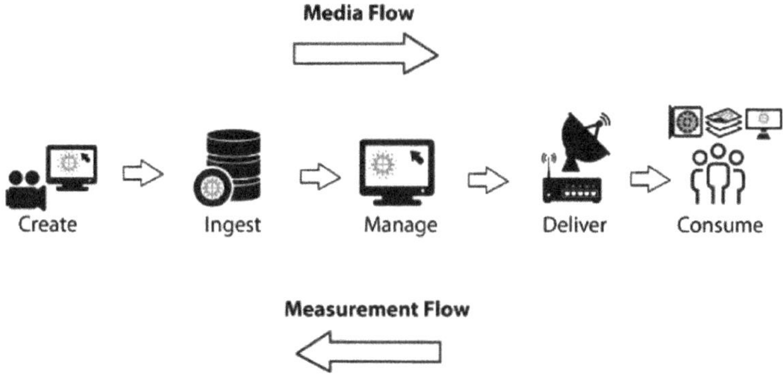

and measurement of consumption and activity constitutes the media supply chain. Within the DAM world, this is a fundamental concept. Like a manufacturing supply chain, successful DAM initiatives seek to minimize the same types of life cycle deviations, errors, waste, and other trouble spots in the media supply chain and seek out remedies.

Departments working in silos will naturally develop processes that work for them, but will create duplicate efforts and costs. Without acknowledging the existence of other departments' needs and potential opportunities the overall enterprise suffers.

If a manufacturing manager were setting up a supply chain it would be foolish to engage with suppliers or sign a contract without first understanding the effect on the rest of the business. The manager may have a gut feeling or know of good suppliers, but each company is unique and needs to maximize profit. There are too many variables that can, left to knee jerk decisions and assumptions, can wreak havoc on the overall performance.

There may be undiscovered opportunities for consolidation improvements, new revenue, or other ventures. The ultimate goal is to improve shareholder value, not make rash decisions, even if everyone is busy or in a survival mode. The same is true in DAM and is another reason for holding off on vendor discussions.

There are several capabilities within a given media supply chain that are important for anyone solving the DAM puzzle to understand. These capabilities are not only helpful to successfully identify an appropriate approach, vendor and system, but how one will affect another. Although some capabilities may not apply to all DAM initiatives, acknowledging what an approach or system does and why it's important or not, is critical.

Regardless of what a media supply chain includes or omits, its success will depend on the quality of its metadata. This is entirely dependent on automation, people and usually both.

Data Follows Workflow

While a company may establish a unified, cross functional strategy, and deploy a DAM system to store assets and provide a unified metadata schema, security, and rights, to support the various media supply chains, it requires workflow. The very nature of the supply chain is how work gets done; assets are developed, approved, and ultimately consumed. Its not only about controlling work steps where appropriate. It's about optimizing the creative output of artists, collective genius of brand managers, development of fresh material and ultimately organizational reach or expansion.

Workflow can be defined simply as increasing the value of work product as it moves from points under management or oversight. To illustrate this, think of the workflow involved to make a peanut butter and jelly sandwich. One could think this is a five-step process:

1. Procure 2 slices of bread, peanut butter and jelly.
2. Spread peanut butter on one slice.

3. Spread jelly on the other.
4. Put the slices together.
5. Cut diagonally in half.

The workflow for making a simple sandwich should be obvious to us. We've done similar things hundreds of times (if not this very morning). However, imagine for a moment that you have no idea of what bread is, or live in a country where peanuts are neither imported nor made into peanut butter? What if to have jelly, one had to locate a berry farm and negotiate a minimum delivery of a bushel of berries you have never heard of, know how to pick the best ones, then cook up a batch? What if wheat was outrageously expensive and wasn't worth making it into bread? Suddenly our workflow of making a simple sandwich becomes far more complex.

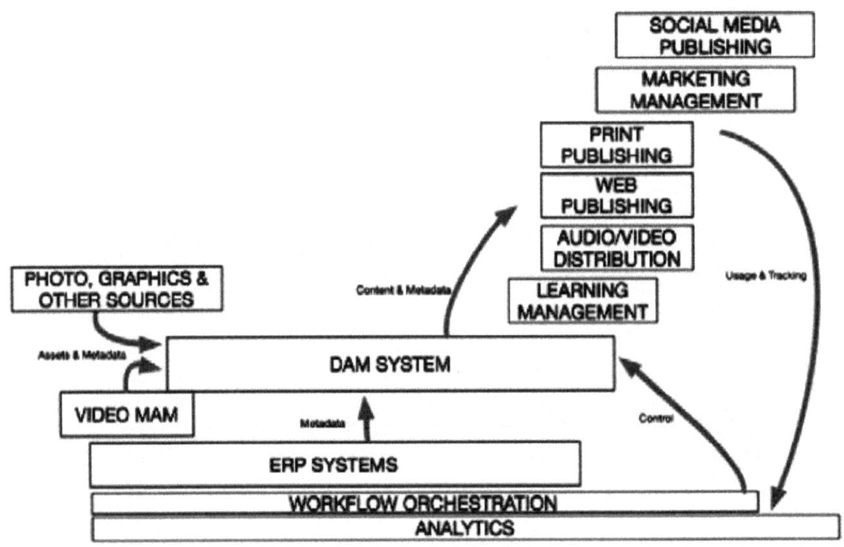

Best Practice for Data Management

We have assumptions and expectations but not using a best practice for workflow and data management creates confusion. We think we know what our media files are, where they are and how to get them. We expect to have ample and easy access to hard drives and networks. We assume everyone should have the right tools for managing data and media files. When these assumptions are incorrect, change or are non-existent, workers become frustrated, confused and sometimes look for someone or something to blame.

Confusion in security, metadata, workflow or any other media supply chain component undermines trust between departments or even staff members on the same team. Mistrust is a key reason large storage arrays and even the best DAM systems go unused. Without proper data management with DAM properly embedded as a fundamental component, the foundation for any digital maturity is inadequate. DAM initiatives are successful when teams work out key processes and build technical platforms on a defined strategy.

It's helpful to understand and work against a model for how DAM supports the Media Supply Chain within these disciplines and platforms.

The trick is to align what stakeholders need and do within the goals of the organization. It's time to work with the borders and edge pieces to the puzzle because this is where we'll find them.

...

A hard drive is not a strategy.

5 FINDING THE EDGE PIECES

The Right Perspective

Saul Steinberg created 85 covers and 642 internal drawings for The New Yorker, including its March 29, 1976 cover, titled "View of the World from 9th Avenue." It was his most recognizable work. The illustration depicts a perspective of New York's 9th Avenue. Up the block is 10th Avenue, then the Hudson River, followed by generalized references to a few major cities across America. A thin stretch of the Pacific Ocean borders loose, almost haphazardly sketched mounds of far flung countries beyond. Its message is clear. To a New Yorker, 9th Avenue isn't the end of the world; that would be anywhere west of 10th. Anyone who has lived in New York understands this instantly.

Numerous periodicals, newspapers, advertising, and even politicians have used or parodied this work of art. The most infamous of these was the poster for the 1984 Robin Williams movie, “Moscow on the Hudson” showing the familiar fonts and pastel colored buildings, only this time with an Eastern view extending to the Kremlin. Steinberg sued Columbia Pictures for copyright infringement and prevailed.

At the risk of suffering a similar fate, the image won't be printed here (a web search would be helpful for this example), but it will be referenced. Beyond the obvious rights management example, Steinberg's illustration provides a larger lesson about those who need a DAM puzzle solved from either a business perspective or for their own jobs: Stakeholders.

One might assume that DAM stakeholders are only the groups of users clamoring for or using a DAM system. However, having some understanding of all stakeholders will not only unlock the value of DAM within an organization, but uncover something of far greater need: strategic insight. Here again, in our daily jobs, it's difficult to manage other stakeholder groups be they far flung or nearby. Most organizations are fraught with silos, busy or apathetic workers, and political agendas. These factors may stand in the way, but they need to be identified and dealt with carefully. With Steinberg's graphic in mind, we can identify three general categories of stakeholders:

The "Here"

These are stakeholders within your immediate department or those with whom you talk or serve regularly. These are people or groups of which there is strong clarity of workflows and media files and easily identified.

The "Near"

There are others such as suppliers or are consumers of our digital media of whom we have a vaguer notion. These stakeholders are connected in some way to your day to day work or occasionally interact. Who they are and with what media supply chains they are dealing would be an educated guess, but can be uncovered through conversations and related teams' knowledge.

The "Far"

Further out is everyone else. These are the stakeholders that might have a significant impact on how assets are created or consumed, but you're not sure. You know they are out there but the level of detail is a mystery. It would take a more serious effort to investigate the media supply chains for these stakeholders. This may have to do with proximity such as those in remote home offices, but many times a "far" stakeholder group is on another floor in the same building or the office down the hall. Ask who, within your enterprise, are in these groups?

Who are your Stakeholders?

Just as in The New Yorker Magazine cover, the detail of your department, the assets you create, manage or deliver, those people who work on your team, are your regular vendors or customers are easily identified (as if they were on 9th Avenue). These are your "here" group.

Identifying Your Stakeholders

Create a list of those groups or departments you are generally familiar, but need to some research to understand more. These are your "near" stakeholders. Finally create a group that you know exist, but have no clue as to what they need or how they operate beyond guessing.

One point to make here is that we ourselves have a bias or perspective of what our DAM problem is and who is affected by it. Another point is we may think we are solving the DAM puzzle for the enterprise, but we could be missing out on greater strategic insight of our organization. We could also be creating more confusion and expense without even knowing it.

What Do Stakeholders Want?

Just as you and your team are beginning to understand who your stakeholders are, it's a fair guess that other groups have their own ideas about DAM and attempts to solve the puzzle themselves. Perhaps they are dealing with asset management processes that are far different than yours. It's important to understand their bias and perspectives as well as your own. They may see their media supply chain and stakeholders differently, and have goals and objectives that may impact your

DAM strategy. Maybe they consider your department in their own "FAR" group, or don't care.

Regardless of the departments listed your three groups, what they want from a media management strategy can vary. For financial managers, it could be to avoid wasted or duplicative investments. Content teams may want to spend more time on being creative. Marketers want to optimize brand building activations. Others would prefer technology that doesn't slow them down.

Each perspective could be important to an initiative. Working with the right stakeholders and bringing them into strategic and tactical groups will determine whether a DAM initiative is successful or not. The best technology could be acquired, metadata could be perfect, and every workflow could be automated, but without governance, the initiative will ultimately erode and fail.

...

6 SMOOTH SURFACES

The "G Word"

Communication and supervision of a DAM initiative by executives and stakeholder groups can be done only through a process known as governance. This is a potential minefield that may cause some stakeholders to react with disdain. It's a topic that has been known to scuttle DAM initiatives if mishandled by executives or stakeholder groups. There are two ways this happens.

The first way is a misunderstanding of what governance is. Governance is a means of managing an initiative through appropriate forums with clearly defined roles and responsibilities. Governance is not synonymous with enforcement, but is strategy in action by stakeholders.

The second way DAM initiatives are threatened is by "governance exhaustion" suffered by many project teams. If every major initiative has a governance team, there is the potential for many opposing priorities and too many meetings yielding few results. Even so, governance for DAM is not only critical for handling various portions of the initiative, but should also evolve into a more extensive foundation for the enterprise as it moves toward digital maturity. This is the ultimate goal actually.

Governance during the planning, design, deployment and maintenance phases, or the lack of it, will determine the success, ongoing health and ultimate adoption of a DAM solution. Without it, the initiative is minimized to an application deployment project. Therefore, it is advisable for organizations to establish effective governing teams at varying levels to include cross-functional stakeholders who can assess, discuss, evaluate, recommend directions, make decisions and keep things on track.

Governance bodies I've helped to create and actually work are made up of sub-teams. Each sub-teams' responsibility, function and composition are highly specific to an organization and therefore, cannot be created generically. However, it is recommended that organizations include executive and content area/subject matter experts as well as organizational and functional managers. This requires IT leadership participation as well, not merely a tech lead or project manager. Appropriate population of groups will ensure the issues (strategic, operational, financial, technical, etc.) be considered within the proper forum and represent the organization well.

Initial goals include:

1. Communicate the mission and charter of the initiative.
2. Ensure DAM as fundamental component within an organization's overall content strategy.
3. Establish goals such as participation, buy in, acceptance and digital maturity.
4. Consolidate digital media management spending into single initiative thereby reducing silos of both technology and budget, or at least understanding the exceptions.
5. Creating momentum for all departments and external partners to utilize a "single source of truth" for digital assets and media workflow.
6. Issues regarding best practices, workflow, operational or features enhancement are managed within the proper framework.
7. An ability to expand the DAM investment ROI by generating greater areas of return in sales, marketing cycle time, business intelligence, and other desired areas that were

previously impossible.

8. Ensuring adoption of new workflows, interfaces, and standards as required by the company and technology platforms.

Governance Planning

Organizations are advised to plan for governance both operationally and strategically to ensure the investment in the DAM platform is continually protected. This goes beyond the difficulties of rolling out a new website.

Holding more training classes or dictating usage cannot achieve the required level of governance when it comes to DAM. One reason for this is that DAM is not a "must use" platform as email or an HR systems are. For example, Creative teams are able to produce imagery or video without a heavy reliance on a DAM system and can continue to remain in tedious, manual workflows, with shared drives and extraneous hard drives. In fact, this is typically their default and most of the time is driven by a lack of trust in any comprehensive solution or platform. As a result, a given teams' adoption of DAM is contingent on their early on-boarding experience and a shared clarity of the benefits of DAM. Without adoption and wide acceptance, a typical corporate culture will not shift.

Governance teams, both at the executive and operational level must understand these factors not just with Marketing or Creative Teams, but across the organization and do so without assumptions or blind expectation. Functioning governance teams deal with the hindrances, conflicts and other factors. Policies and goals can be communicated through this overall forum. DAM is a cross-functional disrupter. I've never seen DAM succeed without governance. Establishing proper governance will create a proven foundation for DAM success. Those that fail to create these structures suffer a more difficult future. These structures can start small and scale up as digital maturity goals increase, but establishing the proper model is key.

Each organization will have its own version of these teams based on the business units, resources and goals. The following teams are recommended:

DAM Leadership: Meets Weekly

- Includes an executive level sponsor, project leads, principal DAM consultant, interested managers, finance and training representation.
- Its purpose is to provide consistent guidance throughout the entire DAM initiative.

IT Team: Meets Weekly

- Includes general IT admin, infrastructure, user access, and help desk support.
- The purpose is to provide technical guidance, support escalation, enforce policies, and ensure availability.

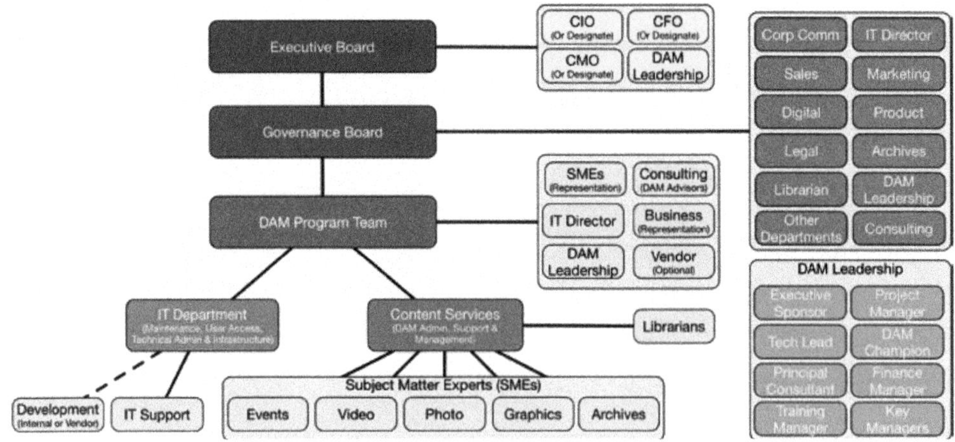

Content Services: New Department/Working Group

- Consists of subject matter expert representatives from photo, video, librarians and other functional and creative groups.
- Provides overall administrative support for DAM operations, modifications, user management and metadata/ taxonomy consistency.

The DAM Program Team: Meets Weekly

- Includes stakeholders from functional teams, IT leads, Consultants, and DAM Leadership.
- The purpose is to provide ongoing oversight on DAM “product” development within the initiative. The team prioritizes feature requests, enhancements, maintenance, and vendor interactions.

Governance Board: Meets Every 2-3 Months

- This is the largest of the teams with participation from all other teams and key stakeholder and business groups.

- The purpose is to facilitate communication, resolve conflict and update strategic and tactical plans.

Executive Board: Meets Every 3-5 Months

- Consists of senior executives and DAM Leadership.
- The purpose is to update executives and solicit feedback on using DAM as a strategic initiative, justify ongoing budget requirements and understand DAM related goals and objectives.

The Mission

Each team has a specific charter but a common mission. The over arching goals are to build and enhance digital maturity within the organization using DAM as the impetus. These groups are designed to promote accountability and transparency and be enforced by the executive team.

With the proper checks and balances across the teams, the organization not only improves its inter-departmental relationships within the DAM initiative, it provides a forum to reduce conflicts. DAM should be the initial and foundation of an organization's digital maturity, but successful governance should eventually shift to a "Digital Governance Model" as soon as DAM is adopted by its stakeholders. The following diagram provides an overview of a governance model.

End User Group Meetings

In addition, it's advised to have bimonthly or quarterly "user groups" meetings. This may be a lunch and learn, a breakfast meeting or something done through an online meeting.

In these, a power user might give instruction on a confusing area or function. The DAM Leadership team may take questions through a chat or text, or the user base can be surveyed on top issues to resolve. This is a great way to not only solicit any issues or requests, but also shows who is not there. Besides reviewing reports showing who has logged into the system, this is a great way to gauge user adoption issues with groups or individuals who may have abandoned the system or initiative.

...

7 THE REFERENCE PICTURE

Hidden Puzzles Revealed

Marketing is the cornerstone of business expansion. I am surprised by organizations that spend vast resources on top staff, innovative product engineering and lean supply chain management only to let it suffer best effort, marketing operations mired in digital survival. Marketing departments are typically main stakeholder groups in a DAM initiative, but often rely on shared servers for storing digital assets and collateral. By improving marketing with DAM, organizations unlock the creativity and effectiveness of their team.

Embedding DAM into product design and innovation oriented teams offer greater opportunities in digital maturity. By providing DAM capabilities to other departments, costs can be reduced and enable sustainable growth. To uncover the opportunities within a DAM initiative for marketing or any other stakeholder group, there is a standard process I use to ensure we're solving the right puzzle and form the foundation for a business case. There are five phases of this analysis:

1. Asset Inventory
2. Workflow Mapping
3. Issue Analysis
4. Resource Review
5. Improvement Thesis

Without this analysis, a business case will suffer from too many intangibles and the initiative will fall into the strong gravitational pull toward a reactive technology deployment. Conducting interviews of various stakeholder groups will allow for a larger understanding of resource utilization and the overall DAM puzzle. This view will provide strategic insight even if the end result is for a single stakeholder group to get things started then potentially add others later. Let's look at an example of this analysis.

Getting to the Truth

A marketing communication team watches a webinar by a DAM vendor and learns what a DAM system does. The team then invites 4-6 team members to an initial meeting to discuss the first 3 phases, the asset inventory, workflow mapping, and issue analysis. The agenda is to uncover what the team defines as an asset, the applications or systems used to manage assets, the workflows within the media supply chain, and some areas of potential improvement.

This is a workshop style meeting and should have some ground rules for allowing open dialogue, confidentiality, honest opinions and safety. Like a conversation with a doctor, DAM initiatives require transparency especially when there are issues to be discussed. While they are the exception, I have witnessed teams within organizations that not only refused to speak to one another, but were outright hostile. Teams often lack trust of both management and other teams for standing in their way to get work done. Sometimes a safe environment is only possible in a one on one meeting. But these usually cover what is supposed to happen and the true nature of the troubling issues within the media supply chain is kept a secret.

Remember that the stakeholders within these groups could be digital natives, tourists or immigrants. They may feel that if their workflows and asset management techniques are discredited or scrutinized, they'll be afraid of the potential outcomes. An atmosphere of fun, trust, and a potential for personal, professional and business improvement must be established and maintained. It is in these meetings that the truth of an organization will be exposed and executives need to be accepting of these issues. I have never been responsible for anyone losing their job because a DAM initiative moved them out. I have however, seen people lose their jobs because they refused to change. It's helpful therefore to focus on the issues, behaviors and practices within media supply chains rather than the personalities of those working in it.

An icebreaker I've used is helpful to get people thinking about working as a team is sometimes required. My favorite is based on the game of Rock, Paper, Scissors. Another one uses small pieces of paper of wildly varying concepts or objects and then I challenge the team to organize them into logical, albeit impossible, patterns. These can be fun ways to kick things off and allows time to observe how the team operates. Once this is done, we need to know what we're dealing with.

The Asset Inventory

Each stakeholder group will hold fast to what's important because they live with a "9th Avenue" perspective. As a result, they will be concerned and interested in providing an inventory of the digital assets they use. Within the workshop, start the process with an asset inventory with a simple list. A design team I interviewed listed these as their assets:

1. Photoshop Graphics
2. Illustrator Files
3. InDesign
4. Templates
5. PDFs
6. Word Documents or Text files
7. Licensed Photography and Imagery

8. Finished and Approved PDFs or InDesign Files
9. Asset Elements such as logos or lines
10. Low Resolution Previews for Approvals
11. Specifically Named Versions related to the Final
12. Archived and outdated material no longer used

Once this step is done to your team's satisfaction, let's look at the user and asset life cycles.

Workflow Mapping: What is Going On?

This leads us into a workflow mapping exercise which may uncover trouble in paradise. It's likely for some who were previously enthusiastic about DAM might suddenly get quiet.

Although we will want to review several workflows, let's start out simple. We need a "primary" workflow. If the group has an asset workflow that is routine, such as the creation of a product brochure, it's helpful to start with something like this and use large wall or a whiteboard.

Across the top of the board, write out the headings of the media supply chain. Take the asset (the result of the primary workflow) in its final form and either write the name of it, or attach it on the whiteboard under Deliver:

Create -> Ingest -> Manage -> Deliver -> Measure

With this in mind, map out the steps to get it into that form be it a final printed document, logo, etc. The discussion of what happens can start anywhere in the process. The goal here is to map out the people, automated or manual steps, systems, dependencies and costs in time or budget to get it done. Having a team develop and comment on the life cycle helps to keep things accurate. Some stakeholders have been known to gloss over the issues. Done effectively, communication opens up and misconceptions or erroneous assumptions are exposed. For example, a designer who names and stores files in a certain shared folder may not know that another designer uploads the same files to a cloud system. Or another may have a cache of logos on her desktop computer for easy access, while another spends hours searching for usable versions every month.

This process is accomplished within a workshop. It's time to walk the stakeholder group through one of their primary workflows and root out the issues such as duplicate efforts, multiple copies of media, manual naming, delivering or organizing assets into folders. The following media supply chain story illustrates how this audit unfolds.

Workflow Audit:
Sales Brochures
Date: March 8
Attendees: DAM Consulting Lead, Mary Smith, George Benson, Rachel West, Bill Shoemaker.

WORKSHOP NOTES:

Mary is a designer who needs to search and use photos as well as upload, edit and provide access to her teams' InDesign documents, PDFs and graphic elements. She usually creates Product Brochures for Product Managers review her work.

In her current process, Mary must go to the Photography department to review available imagery. Each photographer has his or her photos on individual desktops. At one time, the photographers tried to put all of the photos on-line or in a large server, but this was a navigational nightmare. They determined that spending an hour or two with a photographer was easier because he or she could remember where everything was. Of course, Jerry shot about 30,000 photos but since he retired, we don't know what is there.

Some of the older or unused photos are stored in hard drives and arranged by date in a locked cabinet. These drives each have a printed list of the events or subjects on the physical disk for reference. Some of the labels have fallen off. If a photographer is out on a shoot, out sick or otherwise unavailable, Mary must wait until his/her return to access either the desktops or the physical hard drives.

Frequently, she must decide what is going to get the job done. Her options are to purchase (and sometimes re-purchase) stock photography, use what photos she does have (potentially using outdated, unlicensed, or unsuitable imagery), or wait until she can work with the photographer to choose new photos. She decides to wait until the photographer returns.

Two days later, and after sitting with a photographer for two hours, Mary has a few photos for her design. One photo shows a woman's face and she needs to understand any talent and imagery use restrictions with the photography department manager.

She calls but discovers the manager is out on vacation for 3 days. Mary works on the design for a couple of hours, but would like to know if she can use the photo. After 3 days, she gets a call from the photography manager who is "fairly certain" the photo has unlimited usage rights, but she can't find the contract. She says she'll look, but is very busy.

After assuming the rights for the photo is probably okay, Mary returns to her design. Her actual design time so far is 4 hours, but she is interrupted 5 times during that period to help various people with locating other InDesign templates, graphics and other assets. Although this helps others with getting their work done, it wastes 2 hours of her day.

Finally, her design is done and she converts it into a PDF. She emails the PDF to product marketing manager. Unfortunately, the PDF is caught in her out box due to it's excessive size. She doesn't notice until the manager calls her looking for it the next day. She copies it onto a jump drive and walks over to another building to deliver it. The product manager uses the jump drive and tries to open the PDF, but he doesn't have the right version and can't open it. He calls her to re-save it in an earlier version of Adobe Acrobat Reader. Mary has a meeting but returns 2 hours later with the new PDF.

An hour later, the manager has some comments that will be discussed later. He asks if the photos she used are in any other product brochures? She has no idea and will have to get back to him. After multiple emails and calls to other busy designers (wasting over 2 hours of collective work time), she reports, the next day, that a POS (point of sale) poster used one of the photos. The manager is happy with that answer, but still has some changes to make.

So far, this document's creation, management and delivery has taken several hours spread over several days to complete. This process and other issues like them occurs 5-6 times a month to each of the 5 design group staff members when submitting work. The run rate averages 25 brochures/month or 300/year. Product management is only one of several departments that depend on the design team and all are frustrated with the delays, issues overall service level.

Confidential Note to Management: The team is worried that due to the problems, brochures and other work will be outsourced to an agency.

Meanwhile, Back at the Whiteboard

The entire workflow is mapped out on the whiteboard. Each action step is listed along the left and key points are listed within the media supply chain.

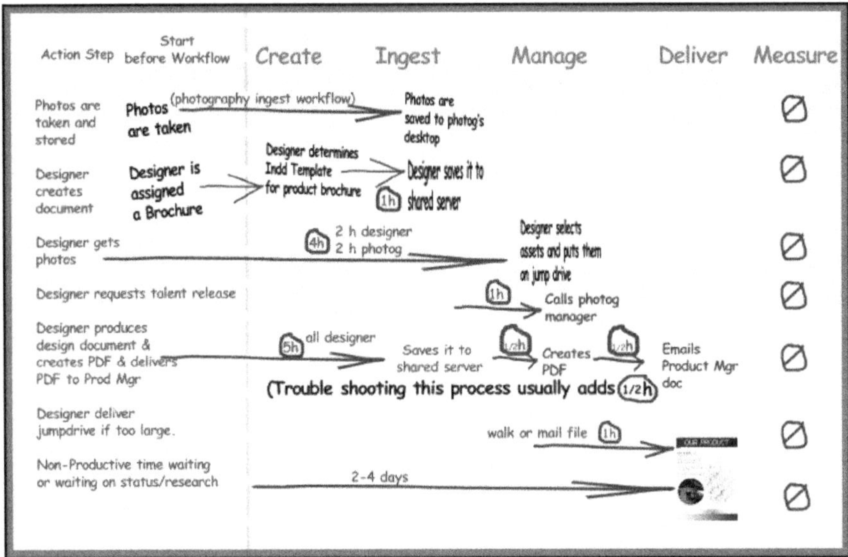

As a workflow is discussed and illustrated, take note of any bottlenecks or duplicative efforts within the process. In the above workflow map, the circled "1h" lets us know this step takes 1 hour. This could be an average of the typical best case time and reasonable worst cases. By including an average time to move each step of the work along, later calculations are much easier. It is necessary to actually prove these, which is the next step. Take some time to measure the process as it really happens. Ensure to test and time several instances of the same workflow. There will be some discrepancies between what is estimated in the workshop and what is observed in a real world situation. In this original workshop estimate, they estimated 13.5 hours per brochure.

With the steps documented, observing the real workflow actually indicated an average of between 9.5 and 10 hours with 5 hours of legitimate design time.

There were several hours that were not accounted for, but can have a tremendous impact on the productivity of the workflow. The hours spent helping other staff with their search and asset management issues, or waiting days for an answer on clearances or access to photographers, had some impact on Mary's creative momentum. I call this out as "also…take a look at these numbers…" It's difficult to include them in a legitimate everyday workflow, but it does demonstrate the larger intangible yet intrinsic benefits of DAM to an organization.

Some issues are "one off" situations such as a product manager's inability to open a PDF. Obviously if there is a PDF reader issue, the first time it happens, the designer may know to save it as an older version the next time. Unless there is some method of ensuring compatibility across all stakeholders, it will happen again. Similarly, if sending large files to other departments is common, the use of jump drives and mailing or walking them across to others should be included. The point is to get initial time estimates, test what is a legitimate process that usually occurs, then add it to the assumption.

In addition to a flow diagram, create an inventory of the components within a workflow. The media supply chain remains on top of this chart, but list all stakeholders, security parameters, systems used, or areas of concern such as

	Create	Ingest	Manage	Deliver	Measure
Assets	Photos PSD AI INDD	AI and PSDs Photos PDFs INDD	InDesign PDF Photos AI and PSDs	PDF	None
Users	Mary Prod Mgmt Photo	Mary Photographer	Mary Photo Manager Photographer	Mary Prod Mgmt	None
Security & Asset Location	Photos in Desktops. Graphics in Shared Drive	Shared Drive folders	Jump Drive (can be lost) Email Shared Drive folder	Desktops Jump Drive	None
Metadata	Project name on files & folders	Name of photos and Indd files	Naming conventions for versions	Email and file naming	None
Systems	Photo Desktops Shared Drive	Shared Drive	Shared Drive Desktop	Email JumpDrive	None
Issues	See Lists	See Lists	See Lists	See Lists	None

manual searching, uploading, and naming conventions. Usually the list of issues is long and requires a "see list" reference. Any "measurement phase" within a current media supply chain prior to DAM practices is usually rare or meaningless, but is worth noting if present or not.

After creating the current state map and chart for the workflows, the team may be tempted to start talking of ways to fix the issues, or worse, about DAM applications. This isn't the time to solve anything; only to map out what the assets are, who touches them, depends on them, what the security issues are, and the systems used even if it's a jump drive. Repeat this for no more than 4 or 5 other primary workflows per stakeholder group.

Once these workflows are mapped (over a single long meeting

or, preferably, over the course of a few workshops), the team should brainstorm and list other workflows such as searching for the right logo, delivery of finished assets to others, and more complex approvals. This exercise will do two things:

1. You will discover other stakeholder groups to interview. Make sure to note any other teams mentioned in the analysis that have an interest in the assets or workflow. These outside teams will be your likely interview candidates. Mary's sales brochure workflow led to a conversation with the photography group.
2. You will educate the stakeholder group. This is where managing change begins. It's tough to get teams to accept change but starting early is always preferred.

These exercises and workshops bring awareness of other teams' problems and modern techniques to solve them. It also will serve to gain user adoption when a system is finally available.

Issue Analysis

With this process mapped out, what bottlenecks or issues can we identify in our workflow with Mary? Were there problems with access, delivery or searching? When the team analyzed this single workflow, this is what resulted:

Issue Analysis for Brochure Design Workflow

1. Assets are locked away in asset owners' desktops or

secured hard drives without access to them with questionable backup.

2. Access is dependent on asset owner's availability and location.

3. Unavailable assets may need to be re-purchased or the stakeholder is forced to reuse photos that don't expand brand voice.

4. Locating the right asset is excessively manual and requires staff input for even the most basic search.

5. Researching rights and clearances is a manual process that may not have a paper trail or validation, or be assumed. This exposes the organization to large infringement fines, especially if rights and talent clearances are clear for one region, but not others.

6. Work time is interrupted with calls to deal with administrative information or staff assistance.

7. InDesign files need to be converted manually to PDFs.

8. Media files need to be delivered to others through a separate system, such as jump drives or email.

9. Large files, typical of media assets, are large and get caught in file size filters creating delays.

10. Manual efforts to deliver media assets are dependent on user availability to convert, save, deliver and ensure file integrity.

11. End user dissatisfaction from non-standard or failed previews.

12. Rework to create a compatible version creates wasted time and requires duplicate manual delivery activities.

13. Research efforts to review asset use in other work is an

arbitrary, manual, process without 100% confirmation of accuracy.

This list was derived from evaluating just a single workflow. There are many other DAM issues that other workflow audits reveal and is a strong reason to interview various teams.

Resource Impact

Review the list with your team and create a table to calculate the issues within the media supply chain to the workflow. For Mary's workflow, we can take the average time (again, the more measured and verified the better) and create a calculation.

We need to gain consensus from the team and eventually, management. Here's our 10 hours of designing a sales brochure workflow and calculating the resource impact stemming from the discovered issues:

Weekly Time Impact for Design Team Workflow for Sales Brochures	Totals	Photographers	Designers	Product Mgmt Team
Research Time		1	1	
Production Time			5	
Review Issues (Not Reviewing)			.5	.5
Rework (Saving, Naming, Reformatting, Conversions)			1	
Delivery Time			1	
Staff Involved/week	6	1	4	1
Brochures/week	5		5.2	
Total Staff Hours to Submit 1 Brochure	**10**	1	8.5	.5
Weekly Staff Hours x 5.2 Brochures	**45.5**	5.2	44.2	2.6
Annual (52 weeks) Hours for 300 Brochures		270.4	2,298.4	135.2
Less Legitimate Production Time	**1500**	--	1500	--
Total Annual Hours Wasted in Sales Brochure Workflow	**1204**	270.4	798.4	135.2
Average Wait Time / Week	**16**		16 Hrs/Wk	
Average Wait Time / Year	**832**		832 Hrs/Yr	

"They have 167 brands and 1 DAM system.
We have 1 brand and 47 DAM systems."
-- Major brand DAM Manager

8 CONSTRUCTING THE BORDERS

Another Workshop for Insight

Within this workshop, several solution categories should be discussed including:

1. User Groups and Roles
2. Security Concerns
3. Workflow Optimization
4. Metadata Needs
5. Consolidation of Systems
6. General Asset Management
7. Best Practices

User Groups

If a DAM system has 1000 potential power users, managing each individual's access to discrete media files would be impossible. To aid in this, user groups, roles and security policies have been the historic, necessary means to manage teams and security for common access or select capabilities.

Organizations have many types of users which may include administrators, product managers, designers, video editors, photographers, managers, and external users such as agencies, PR, press outlets or production studios. Each group will need to have access to a single asset or collections of assets and no access to others. Some assets may only be viewable by a group without download capability while other errs may download a low resolution version. Files that are embargoed may only be seen by legal and invisible to everyone else. A new product sales brochure may be accessible by everyone. Each asset will have a security policy that coordinates the user group's access to it (see it, not see it), and what those users can do with it (download it, view only, export it, edit it). Again, security is different from "rights" which indicate what a user can do with it once they have it.

Specific users are grouped by business oriented requirements and within a structure to support it. A photography user group would hold all of the photographers for example.

Internal users would be grouped as such, external users in the External Users Group and both would be included in the

Everyone Group. DAM systems should distinguish internal from external users, create a hierarchy of user groups with cascading access, or, within better systems, use a robust directory service that manages more unique needs.

To illustrate how user groups and roles work, assume a company creates user groups in this hierarchy:

- EVERYONE>
  - Internal Users>
    - Administrators
    - IT
      - Development
      - Help Desk
      - Project Management
    - Marketing
      - Marketing Communications
      - Product Marketing
      - Corporate Marketing
      - Digital
      - Web Team
      - Social Media
      - Advertising
    - Sales
      - Sales Operations
      - Account Management
    - Production
      - Video
      - Photography

Design

Events

Product Management

Customer Service

Human Resources

Training

External Users>

Agencies

Ad Agency A

Ad Agency B

Photo Agency

Video Production Agency

Press Outlets

CNN

Yahoo

Post Newspaper

Customers

As individual users accounts are created either manually or by directory service import, they should be assigned to user groups. A best practice is to integrate an organization's email/ employee/HR directory to the DAM directory in order to instantly maintain authorized users. This avoids former employees from accessing the system should it be served from outside a corporate firewall. Where external users need access to the system, these accounts must either be maintained within a similar directory service, sometimes separate from a corporate employee directory, or individually. Larger enterprise environments may offer a vendor ID or similar that provides limited access to corporate systems for contractors or other groups. These temporary IDs directories are excellent methods for accessing DAM systems and should be encouraged with IT.

Corporate directories, such as LDAP (Lightweight Directory Access Protocol) may include information such as user name, password, email or other light contact information. More robust directories include an employee's region or country, office, department, supervisor, and role. Where these values exist, they should be considered as DAM user groups are developed. There are several reasons for this, but primarily to help with administrating the potential complexity of specific user groups and roles. As users are created in the corporate directory with details about region, job title, etc., these may be mapped to a DAM user directory to automatically assign user groups and roles.

User Roles

A user's "role" indicates the level of administration an individual has. Here are some sample roles we might use in a system:

Read Only

A "read-only" role (or casual user) allows for the search and previewing of assets without any provision for download. Users may be limited to a "casual" interface to avoid licensing of more advanced administrative interfaces or training needs.

Standard User

This role usually provides for search, preview, download, export and may participate in workflows. Some assets may be specifically tagged as read only, which may limit these users' activity. This role usually accesses the main administrative interface, but will have limited edit capability.

Editor

Editors have the ability to upload, edit and change security policies for assets along with Standard User capabilities. Generally, editors work within a user group or groups within the main administrative interface. Assets uploaded by an editor are usually fully maintained by that editor or other editors with permission.

Group Administrator

This role allows certain users to administrate access for user groups they manage. Generally, group administrators mayadd other users to or remove users from their own group. They may have overall edit capability for any asset that is managed by their group. This is especially helpful in remote offices so that the dependency on HQ based administrators is reduced. Group administrators have access to all interfaces including an "admin interface" which is behind the scenes to make limited changes.

Super Administrator

This user has god-like powers to manage any user, group, security policy, assets or workflows. It is advised to create super administrators outside of standard directory based users so that mundane day to day use of the system doesn't make significant or destructive changes to the system. Super Admins have access to the admin interface as well as all others. They can delete anything.

Workflow Improvement

With our map of this excessively manual process and issues list, brainstorm recommendations on improvements. Here is the list generated by the team with a DAM consultant to generate a future state using best practices and fundamental DAM technology:

1. Assets should be saved in a central location and available to authorized users.
2. An asset's owner should be entered into metadata, and be a required field. This information helps to clarify the asset's origin or other questions. An asset owner may be a department.
3. The most recently acquired assets should be shown first in a search.
4. All photos, including stock and contracted, should be grouped in categories of place, photographer, year, product and other taxonomies.
5. Appropriate metadata should be added by the photographers, designers and other authorized users to ensure they are returned when searched.
6. Searches should be able to be saved by a user for later as new assets arrive.

7. Designers need a way to review rights metadata, browse, download, and convert the files into other formats as required.
8. Rights limitations and terms of use are clearly indicated on respective assets during browse, search results, metadata, and need to be accepted by the user prior to download or export.
9. Questions should be referred to the metadata on any asset.
10. Photographers and some designated designers should be allowed to make edits to an asset.
11. InDesign files and other documents should have a way to be converted into a PDF.
12. PDFs converted from InDesign files should maintain a relationship to the original design document and a link to allow other users gain access to it.
13. There is only one version of any one asset at any time within the system regardless of its size.
14. Users who send files to others should have a simple process for sending a link to the asset. These links should be able to be sent to both internal and external users without having to go through major hoops.
15. Users will be notified that the asset was successfully delivered and opened.
16. Any link for review of an asset would provide a thumbnail upon initial review, a preview medium resolution, and the original file which can be previewed within the browser. This alleviates the need to download and launch a 3rd party application and incompatibility issues.

17. Converted versions may be exported by trained users.
18. Any photo or graphic that has a relationship to another document or presentation should be able to be reviewed.
19. Placed graphics in particular should display all InDesign files in which it has a relationship.

Mary would be assigned to the Design user group and her role would be Editor. As a result, she can upload media assets, edit metadata and assign them into categories. She can manage security policies on those as well. She creates an InDesign document that will need graphics, text and photography. She would also be assigned to the Photography user group, but have a role as a Standard User. As such, she can browse assets that she can read and download. She creates a light box collection (a shopping cart), of photos she may want to use.

Mary could download the collection to her desktop, but this would create alternate copies and add to her backup. Instead, because she uses InDesign, she can use a plug-in (from within InDesign and provided by the DAM vendor), to import specific photos from her DAM system directly into her document. This forms a relationship the DAM system can track between the photo and the InDesign document. Some systems provide access to DAM elements using a small application such as Adobe Drive or similar "drive mapping" tool. This places a virtual drive on a user's desktop to access assets as if it were in a shared folder. This can be a good compromise for users who don't want to log into a system and prefer shared folders.

The benefit is all assets are managed as if they were uploaded and downloaded in the DAM system instead of being stored in a specific folder.

Mary accesses the DAM system again for graphic elements she needs. She searches and finds an asset that has an incorrect description. Because she has an Editor Role, she can correct the description and save it. She then selects two graphics and imports those into her document, again using the plug in. Mary launches Photoshop and creates a new graphic for her design. She places the graphic into her document, this time without using the plug-in because the original graphic is not in the DAM system.

In due course, she places the photos and graphics she imported, then adds text. She saves the InDesign document directly into the DAM system using the plug in (or mapped drive).

Workflow Automation

The DAM system should handle this process in the following manner:

1. Create Import the InDesign file into the DAM system as an .INDD file.
2. Maintain the relationship between the graphics already in the system and NOT upload them into again.
3. Import the graphic Mary created as a NEW asset and maintain the relationship to the design document.

4. Create a low resolution thumbnail of the InDesign document used as a reference during search results.
5. Create a mid level resolution PDF that includes each page, page size, is color correct and linked to the InDesign document.
6. Provide a method for Mary to add metadata to both the uploaded InDesign file and the graphic she created in Photoshop.
7. Provide a method for Mary to add a security policy to the graphic so that only her Design user group may download it and internal users may only see it, while external users may not see it.

She will then add a security policy to the InDesign file so that only the Design user group may see it and download it. Because she has an Editor role in the Product Marketing user group, she can upload finished documents for review purposes and adds a security policy to the PDF so that Product Management may see and download it.

Through this process, we accomplish several things:

1. We uncover the various asset life cycles.
2. We identify the key stakeholders.
3. We map the issues within a workflow.
4. We call out areas of waste.
5. We generate possible solutions guided by practical experience.
6. We optimize the workflows.

7. We generate requirements based on real world needs.

At this point, we can begin to see a new picture forming. Through team building, discussions of problems and solutions services to create a strategic plan of DAM and ultimately digital maturity. The analysis must be presented to executives, our governance teams, and our here, near and far stakeholders. How the puzzle, pieces and reference picture are presented to them will, again, endanger the initiative to foster a digital maturity road, or be mired in a technology buy.

...

9 WORKING THE INTERNAL PIECES

The Heart of the Puzzle

Simon Sinek, one of the most popular speakers on TED.com, has explained, in simple terms, why the great leaders and motivators are effective at persuasion and others are not. His central message is there are three aspects to inspire change: The "Why, How, and What." Those that have had extraordinary success, such as Apple or Nike, started from the "Why", then moved to the "how," then to the "what." His belief is people don't buy "what" you do; they buy "why" you do it. This is true in building a business case for DAM. Most people, including DAS aficionados, focus on the "What" and explains their minimal success when justifying a DAM system.

Requesting budget for another hard drive is focusing executives on "the what" you do (I need to store stuff). DAM however, requires more justification due to the resource impact and the potential for strategic improvement. DAM needs an elevated, inspirational justification to move beyond the technology and workflows.

Sinek's focus on the "why" first, then the "how", then the "what" helps us to model our case for an investment in a DAM initiative. Without this approach, the justification can be tough otherwise. Consider the following approaches and estimate the amount of the budget request an executive might expect to receive:

Scenario 1:
"I need a DAM system to store our media files better so we can all find them and we won't waste so much time. We are getting so many videos, photos and graphics every day. Marketing is always complaining that everything is so disorganized and they spend a lot of money on recreating media. I need DAM to do my job better and the company will work better. We will save lots of time and expense. Let me show you the technology I need."

Scenario 2:

"We want to improve our shareholder value and leadership in our industry. As our industry becomes more reliant on digital media and operations, we need to mature digitally as a company. We need greater insight into our company performance and want our employees, partners and customers to have a great experience with us.

We want to increase our brand value while reducing exposure to lawsuits. Through this, we'll serve our stakeholders and customers more effectively, enjoy greater operational efficiency which will speed our time to market. We'll have greater control over our brand and increase its value with our customers and partners. Let me show you our strategic digital initiative proposal based on our cross-functional research.

Clearly the second approach will lay a foundation for a larger budget. Any investment in storage based on a need to store an overwhelming number of media files (and the endless duplicates) will not justify a high dollar amount. This is a DAS approach. Many organizations, with a DAS view, will focus the problem and solution on technology and fail to acknowledge many of the needs and non-technical costs.

Without executive buy-in, a unified strategy for digital maturity and proper governance in place, this case for DAM is far more difficult because it speaks to the "what" of DAM.

Keys to the Benefits

There are 4 main areas to keep in mind when looking for possible benefits. These were first introduced to me by Michael Moon (1):

1. *Poor Processes*

Even with existing systems there is a lack of streamlined process integration of media elements (raw media, finished assets, etc.) to stakeholders including marketing departments, legal, creative services and others to satisfy requirements and market demand. The lack of a uniform understanding and reporting of workflow and media related project activities, collaboration create road blocks and brand inconsistencies. Consequently, designers and/or content owners have little to no quality control which neither identify weaknesses or how to resolve them. Poor processes don't allow for the fulfillment of business outcomes.

2. *Weak Collaboration*

Among key contributors a media supply chain such as creative services and marketing communication, weak collaboration yields work of lower quality reflecting the nature of either local or geographically distributed teams that must either coordinate or recreate countless production activities. Coordination of this type constitutes hundreds or thousands of peer-to-peer interactions and communications (emails, phone calls, instant messenger, spreadsheets) that are difficult to achieve across

(1) With credit to Michael Moon at GISTICS

multiple time zones and locations. Ongoing status reviews, commentaries, questions, and approvals of work in process become the bottlenecks or constraint on productivity. The result is time delays, overtime, and staff frustration due to pressured deadlines and late night or home based catch-up or, as in the case of legal review of photographs, the abandonment of the approval entirely.

3. Orphaned Content

This constitutes acquired media files such as photographs or layouts that a company has lost, misplaced or housed in an unreachable server or desktop, demanding that potential users or designated staff spend extra time calling others or searching for the file themselves in computers, tapes, physical binders and other libraries. Often the search is abandoned altogether and the needed asset is recreated. Orphaned content is emphasized by having a centralized collections of media elements, templates, and finished goods but having at least 10 other potential areas for media assets.

Most if not all offer inadequate search technologies to retrieve preexisting media or templates. These inadequacies compound a larger, more expensive problem: version control and the inability to maintain parent-child relationships between a source file, its derivatives and renditions and the specific legal rights with which it is limited. A company's orphan content results in massive duplication of effort, needless direct expenses, and inconsistencies of the brand voice.

4. *Islands of Automation*

These entail the organically grown bottom-up technical systems that essentially do similar things, but are used by independent departments or stakeholders within the company. As in the case of existing systems, it uses a proprietary interface and is limited in which formats it supports. This system doesn't interoperate sufficiently with existing product databases, share processes or yield consistent activity/use data. The largest hidden cost of this issue lies in a lack of responsiveness to market opportunities, quickly understanding legal exposure, and brand consistency.

Each of these four factors contributes to a debilitating cycle of inefficiencies, revenue suppression and cost burdens. Existing systems are part of an unwitting but "organic" strategy that has emerged as the only repositories for digital imagery. A legitimate media supply-chain strategy for digital content constitutes a

A systematic approach for integrating "good" workgroup automation with a unified technical infrastructure, based on a business strategy.

This strategy should place an emphasis on resolving the above four factors within a central digital asset management system, extending it both technically and functionally to the enterprise.

DAM: A better way to sell more _______?

In any organization, you will engage executives who will want to know how an investment in DAM will help expand the business, not to do a job better. This is a core point of the business case and one that must be developed properly. Here again, communication and leadership is required. Unconsciously, executives will need to have confidence in the arguments or the approval for the initiative may suffer delays or lose out to other projects. Our task is to educate, communicate and propose DAM as a business enabler that's worth the trouble if done correctly. Executives will have questions about costs, ownership and many others. We need to have the answers.

How Much is DAM?

What do executives consider to be expensive? For some large organizations I've worked with, $50,000 is a lot because they have the Digital Asset Storage (DAS) view. Other companies approve as much as $10 million for their DAM budget. Is this a matter of having deeper pockets or trusting executives? The answer is value rather than cost. If I ask for a $1 in investment and I can prove that I'll return $2, is there a good chance the proposal will be approved? The key to unlocking this question is understanding an executive's mindset around investments. Too many business cases are centered on what DAM will do. Costs will go down! Everyone will be more efficient! Processes will improve! These on their own are not compelling arguments. They do not communicate either financial or strategic value. A business case needs both.

The Elusive ROI

If you request budget for an investment, a CFO will want to understand ROI in terms he or she wants, not yours necessarily. There are various approaches in use today, but a popular method CFOs use to evaluate investments is through the firm's cost of capital or weighted average cost of capital (WACC). A company's cost of capital is considered to be the return rate the organization could earn if it used money for an alternative investment with the same risk. Put another way, the cost of capital is the opportunity cost of investing money for a specific purpose.

There is usually a "hurdle rate" a business case must offer as minimum benefit, but this number is only part of the story. If this hurdle rate is reached by your financial projection, this will only get you "on the golf course." There are still a lot of "shots" to make and, like golf, these benefits will determine the outcome.

Getting to the Real Benefit

The benefits of DAM are wide and can be proposed in different categories. The categories used and measured in a proposal however will directly characterize how much that benefit is worth to a CFO against other competing project initiatives. Which initiative wins will be based on an equation continually running through a CFO's mind. What are these categories of benefit and how does this equation work?

Better Creative Work

Even if a company appreciates creative improvement, proposing a DAM system to help win creative industry awards will offer a CFO about 97¢. There are better ways to improve creativity in a firm such as hiring talented artists or creative directors.

Process Improvement

In our earlier workshops, we saw how an analysis measured areas of waste. DAM is about unlocking the value of an optimized workflow. Even with a good hurdle rate, a DAM initiative may, for example, compete with a proposal for a workflow management system tied to a content management system (not that this will solve the puzzle). This alternative investment in other platforms could be compelling to executives given the choice. As a result, consider a $1 investment in process improvement will only return that same $1 to the CFO.

Cost Reduction

Process improvement will most likely save money, but there are other areas including avoiding uncontrolled storage costs, reducing legal exposure, or shipping costs. However, these costs are usually relegated to be a result of poor management or staff performance. This will call into question things that have everything to do with a lack of a DAM initiative, but not point to DAM as the solution. Although these are important, CFOs will generally have little regard for them as the primary basis for an initiative. More often they'll want to reduce headcount, reduce technology investments, and/or renegotiate vendor contracts. Although these are strong areas for cost reductions by executives, they can be far more disruptive than a strategic DAM initiative in the long run. Generally, a $1 investment in cost reduction will offer a CFO $2 in return.

The justifications appear to be poor returns on investment from a financial perspective but are in wide use by DAM program teams and champions. However, they remain critical for any business case. On their own though, they will not be enough to close the value equation for compelling approval. What are the categories that are not only more compelling, but might even get you an invitation to lunch in the executive dining room?

Improved Sales

Imagine your company grows at 10% each year, has a net income of $4M on revenue of $25M in total sales, and 25 sales people. Your 200 knowledge workers are engaged in sales, marketing, legal, support and production. Your research shows each of them, on average, spends at least 6 hours per week in various tasks (the industry average) including searching cloud sites and hard drives for marketing collateral and other media, converting, answering status questions and other non-productive tasks as compared to what a DAM initiative would deliver.

You've also uncovered through your governance team, that for every sales person who is hired, they bring in an average of $160,000 in net income. Your sales director wants to hire more account executives, but marketing needs better tools and legal needs more help due to their workload, including a frivolous but potentially expensive copyright infringement case.

If 200 knowledge workers spend 6 hours/week in tedious, non-productive time due to a lack of proper media management, this equates to 60,000 hours annually, or the equivalent of 28 FTEs [(200 workers x 6 hours/week x 50 weeks) /2080 hours/ year].

Working with the CFO, you've agreed on a conservative labor rate of $20/hour as a way of attaching a value to this waste. Even at this low rate, this equates to the company funding $1,200,000 for wasted work time each year.

The sales improvement category however is not based on removing 28 FTEs (this issue is spread across the organization rather than direct individuals), but to reorganize a company's digital strategy to recoup that productivity through DAM, create enterprise improvements and fund sales improvement.

As a result, marketing would enjoy a higher level of digital capability. Legal will have an audit trail for rights managed material. In addition to more staff, sales will have better, more targeted marketing activations and up to the moment product imagery.

Projecting this further, financial models indicated that a DAM initiative of $500,000 investment each year for three years would not only add 10 sales executives, but generate an extra $400,000 in profit.

Your company may not have 200 knowledge workers but far more. This equation at 2000 knowledge workers will recoup the productivity of nearly 192 people. DAM, in tandem with analytics and continuous on-boarding of stakeholders are the puzzle pieces that bring about digital maturity. When the digital conversation is managed through an efficient means of media workflow and technology, the results measured and refined, the constraints to productive revenue generation are mitigated.

This is the narrative that uses the other components as not the main arguments, but as proofs. This is only one facet but there are many other examples to research and develop. Rely on your governance team to help uncover these. Your sales, finance and marketing team should develop a model to understand where marketing activations result in measurable leads and sales. This model would then project where marketing cycle time improvements will result in more sales.

Where sales presentations are outdated or incorrect, DAM provides a measurable way to make instant corrections, updates and delivers them effortlessly. Companies that outsource media creation and delivery can take DAM in-house to reduce their spend on wasted inefficiency and improve their own competitive advantage based on a renewed digital strategy. Agencies looking to create new revenue streams can offer this as a service to their clients. To a CFO, improved sales will return $100 for that $1 investment.

Improved Shareholder Value

If there is one category that demonstrates the maturity of a business case, it's improving the stock price or shareholder equity. Beyond an improvement in operations and profitability there are other, value driving benefits that are less obvious. Even with a break even ROI with an investment in DAM, a firm will be able to be nimbler in responding to shifts in a market. As crowds move from Facebook to something not yet invented, marketing and sales teams will merely have to "add" a few metadata fields and delivery options. This will avoid the science fair projects when rallying for new opportunity.

A company that demonstrates digital maturity with its metadata, workflow and measurable on boarding of stakeholders in order will be more attractive for acquisition than one that does not. A firm that has moved beyond digital survival to maturity will be able to lead markets in ways beyond the edges of their puzzle as we'll see later. To offer a CFO a business case that demonstrates how DAM improves shareholder value will turn his $1 into $1000.

Persuading Executives

The company needs a DAM initiative as a pathway to digital maturity that yields profitability and value. Armed with a variety of stakeholder views and metrics of the issues, examples of solutions, and both a strategic and financial ROI, it's at this point the team is ready to make the case based on the "why."

In the more successful initiatives in which I've worked, the business case was presented as a "case of cases" from the various stakeholder groups rather than within a single department. Departments developed and communicated, from their own perspective, how DAM would improve sales operations, profitability and would support future business initiatives. Some of the individual departments would use a DAM initiative to improve sales, others offered cost and time improvements based on research. At the end, a summary of strategic and financial benefits was outlined. The DAM puzzle was described as something far more widespread than a media file storage problem. With an executive sponsor, IT and cross functional governance teams advocating to solve the DAM puzzle, the CIO, CIO and other executives were compelled to listen. With this knowledge, executives came the realization that they had a "fiduciary responsibility" to solve for a strategic DAM initiative, rather than remain in DAS, digital survival, and the productivity and profitability hindrances.

This approach relied on trust and transparency. But it also had to do with understanding the mindset of the executive and establishing rapport.

Who owns a DAM initiative?

At it's core, this question is primarily about funding and secondarily, about management. The answer will vary within different organizations. Where there is a strong tech team over executive information management, a lack of cross functional buy-in on strategy and governance, or strong adherence to traditional corporate departments, executives will look to place this in a departmental silo.

Our goal is digital maturity based on comprehensive user adoption in DAM technologies and practices. Stuffing everything into a silo won't achieve this. If the foundational principles are in place, DAM will naturally be owned by the governance team or a consortium of departments (yes, including the IT department). Where digital asset management has been properly advocated, executives will, in some cases, look to fund the initiative through a corporate budget to get things going. At some point, the initiative may be funded through individual department allocations, but this decision will vary by firm.

The Anatomy of a Business Case for DAM

As with any puzzle, it's helpful to have a reference picture as a guide. Below is a list of areas typically used in a business case "package." This should also provide a reminder of areas sometimes forgotten by those new to business cases. It's helpful to think of this as a package of 3 main points:

The Strategic Roadmap

This includes an executive summary and general overview to orient the reader to the main objectives, background considerations, and the basics of the other sections in the business case. It's highly likely few will make it beyond these few pages. The following are sections to expand beyond the summary.

The Strategic View

This section is helpful to define areas discussed in previous chapters and personalized to the organization based on identified real world statistics and use cases. For example, if your company has a pervasive DAS approach that has created bottlenecks and silo's which can be measured, this is like gold.

In my experience, anecdotes and common examples which are blatantly counter to company mottos or rhetoric are particularly powerful. Is your company "Positioned for Greatness?" How many systems are used to store, manage or deliver media, metadata, or both? How much is this costing the organization in time and expense? What are these efforts giving your company besides a way to speed up a manual process? How great is that? The point is there is a strategic issue in your company and it will take a strategic solution to solve it. These should include:

The Need for Digital Maturity in the Company

This should illustrate how DAM offers a strategic pathway to the company's content and digital strategy and the need for it. How has the lack of DAM operational practices and technical systems limited the company's capability or market response? What are some of the DAS vs DAM examples? What has been done that either doesn't work or is unjustifiable to continue. What strategic improvements could be realized?

The Initiative as a Platform

The DAM initiative is not only about selecting and justifying a technology investment, but seeks to shift the organization toward digital maturity. Users will continually want to know about interfaces, specific capabilities, and whether it's served in the cloud. The DAM initiative will, through a natural process, move from being an abstract hope to, not an application, but an attractive platform. This lessens the focus on a DAM application and elevates the conversation to be a cross functional, multi-faceted, 21st century solution.

The Core Business Case

After the workshops have been completed, there should be ample examples and issues to list. In each example, a department should provide a brief use cases, a time and cost impact, and a list of systems that a department uses. It's also helpful to list what options the department has or could consider for resolving the issues.

Departmental Business Needs

Although this should be a cross functional initiative, the needs of DAM, like Speaker Tip O'Neill said about politics, are local. DAM happens in the editing suite, the photo studio, or the production office. This is a list of the non-technical business needs each department has. It's effective to group these in terms of common needs by separate departments, areas that will reduce costs, improve operations per company mission or vision, and other benefits.

Future State by Department

What are the workflows that are affected by department and

what are the measurable differences? What improvements reduce bottlenecks, increase efficiency, and speed an individual media supply chain? Each department, within its own business case, will show a variety of benefits based on their evolution using DAM practices.

DAM Requirements

This section provides an overview of the individual needs of each department that point to features and capabilities of a technical platform or how the organization itself needs to change because of it. It is within this section that different asset types, workflows and approaches may create a divergence from other departments. For example, a video department may need to create a complete video clip library for their producers and editors. Photographers will need a way to rate, add metadata, create catalogs and contact sheets. Music teams will need instant audio playback and organization. Print design teams need InDesign support, placed graphics linking, and automatic PDF creation. Intuitive, customizable user interfaces are usually the single most important component. As of this writing, few systems are able to accommodate all of these needs regardless of vendor's best efforts.

A list of overall system needs will be created and listed by categories pertaining to metadata management, workflow automation, user management and delivery options. The research should indicate the most common needs across all departments and thus provide a weight to be used during later evaluations. Keep this list handy for the next chapter.

Implementation Planning

Based on the departmental needs, requirements and weight scores, the governance team must prioritize the phases of the initiative. Through these sometimes lively discussions, a roadmap of investment, changes to workflows, asset life cycles and media supply chains, as well as user groups to onboard will be developed. It is extremely helpful to solicit the services of a DAM practitioner to facilitate these discussions. Media management systems, as stated previously, have a core DNA that services video, photo and other asset types and workflows. A DAM practitioner will guide the DAM requirements into the correct system type. In addition, it's imperative to outline existing asset migration. The only way a DAM system gains trust by users is through having actual assets available. An asset migration phase will require its own prioritization by the program team.

Change Management and Communications Plan

Change management should start the minute a DAM program team decides to create an initiative. It is usually the most difficult part of DAM. While this is a responsibility of governance teams, communication plans are critical to maintain enthusiasm, buy-in, and interest at all levels. A program team may establish a DAM program office to facilitate ongoing communication, questions, and schedules.

Within this office, a DAM team will construct a RACI chart to document the stakeholders, individual departmental leads, roles and responsibilities. RACI is an acronym used establish who within the stakeholder group will be (R)esponsible, (A)ccountable, (C)onsulted, or (I)nformed. Governance team members are also indicated on the Governance team chart.

Branding the Platform

A change management practice that has proven to be effective is to brand the platform with a personality or name that draws attention, interest and establishes the eventual system for its users.

In one case, a DAM governance team discussed the qualities they wanted in the platform. Attributes such as being something to be relied on, was helpful in fetching/retrieving assets, and being friendly to its users were discussed. One particularly creative person said it sounded like a dog. The archivist on the team did some research and discovered that the founder of the 60-year-old firm had a Boston Terrier. The team named the system after the canine.

Whenever a user received an email from the system, it appeared as if the sender was the dog, complete with a caricature and paw print signature. The users of the system identified the initiative and platform with the dog, allowing for the team to send emails, make improvements or even swap out core technologies without undermining the established goodwill, governance, communication and change management. At a large internal event, the team rented a

Boston Terrier to spread both awareness and the brand of the DAM platform.

Other companies, typically beholden to acronyms have used DAMP (Digital Asset Management Platform) as a way to avoid an otherwise unsavory term not appropriate for a religious organization or CAL (Company Asset Library). Others name the platform after random animals such as Red Squirrel, or objects tied to a film studio such as “The Slate.”

These recommendations can be very positive for supporting the idea and availability of a DAM system, but they are not only designed to engage and guide. There are situations the team will encounter that will test the effectiveness of the communication and change management. Change management will be needed to enforce changes to achieve the goals outlined. For example, during the research it may be discovered that a number of shared servers and cloud sites are in heavy use. Based within the DAM strategy, these servers and sites would be required to be decommissioned in order to achieve the benefits.

It’s interesting how the same users who support the idea of a DAM system will also fight to maintain a shared G: Drive or cloud box.

Time Line and Schedule

This section creates a Gantt chart of major milestones for the initiative as understood by the team. This time Line will be refined as the team selects a vendor and priorities. In addition to selection, design, testing and launch estimates, a schedule of governance and departmental communications will be outlined.

Conclusions and Recommendations

This sums up the business case as a final argument and recommends the project toward a next step which is to approve the initiative. Be sure to include a sign off sheet for your governance teams and executives.

Analysis Backup

This organizes the research of business and feature needs, workflows, asset types, metadata, users and stakeholders, and proposed media supply chain issues/improvements.

It was a venture capitalist who told me that if you want investment, ask for advice. If you ask for money, all you'll get is advice. Advice from executives then is best sought prior to submitting the business case. The goal is to get a reality check from the executive sponsor and governance teams with actual costs. If the business case projects that a DAM initiative will generate a significant amount of savings and improve sales, or even affect the bottom line, these assumptions and estimates should be discussed in advance. Meetings with the CIO and CFO and the executive sponsor is highly encouraged to ensure that any technical and financial assumptions are sound or policies maintained. This provides an excellent opportunity to meet, establish rapport and improve buy-in without asking for money.

The last page of the business case is a sign off sheet for your stakeholder groups if required and governance team, and overall project signatory. Your company may have specific documents or spreadsheets that are used to manage project submissions either in electronic form or paper.

Now that many of the pieces are place, let's look at who and what will get the puzzle solved.

...

"I've been in IT for 20 years and I've never heard of DAM. Are you sure it's a real thing?"
- Insurance company CIO

10 GETTING HELP FROM PUZZLE MASTERS

Bringing in the Fresh Fish

Given the choice between wild caught salmon and farm raised, I usually choose fresh, wild caught. It may be an unreasonable bias, but to me the taste is better. These fish have my respect. They were out in the open sea, fighting for food, and surviving on their instinct. I don't know if they have memory, but they had to learn how to live in the wild and avoid predators. The thought of farm raised salmon swimming in the same water with the same fish for months or years while gorging themselves on pellet and vitamins isn't that appealing to me.

In my experience, companies have similar issues when it comes to DAM initiatives. Program teams are established by champions looking to make a change, but in many cases, those with any type of media management knowledge have been, like the farm raised salmon, swimming in the same water with the same fish for a long time. They don't know what is happening in other waters or where predators are lurking. Unless an organization has a “fresh” DAM practitioner on retainer or staff, the program team will suffer from a lack of awareness of best practices, options and insider secrets. Again, a tech team mentality is a dangerous pond in which to swim.

There are DAM experts who know how to avoid danger and thrive in any environment with a commitment to success in DAM. Some of these experts are consultants, others are vendors of DAM systems or DAM services such as rights management, metadata curation, language translation and many others. Selecting puzzle masters for your DAM initiative can be challenging, especially with respect to DAM vendors. Here are a few things to consider.

DAM Consultants: Agnostic and Otherwise

No two companies need exactly the same technology, governance, metadata or workflows. DAM consultants who are committed to appropriately serving their clients cannot be beholden to a vendor or cookie cutter solutions. There are technology agnostic consultants and there are vendor consultants who only work with one application. Vendor consultants, while certainly knowledgeable about their chosen application, will not provide as many options or insight as some agnostic ones. Like a hammer that sees every problem as a nail, vendor consultants will be tempted to force all DAM requirements into their single application.

If a vendor's project manager is the primary consultant on the project, there is a limit to how much he or she can offer. The goal for a vendor consultant is to ensure that the system delivers the capability that is ordered. Items such as governance, business alignment to a digital maturity strategy, or change management are secondary. Yet these are critical to the success of the initiative. The vendor consultant is paid to provide (through a tech team mentality) the ordered technology, but it will be up to you to figure out the rest.

In my experience, DAM consultants should be vendor agnostic and have a wide purview of systems, methods, best practices, and options. Better agnostic consultants have worked in the trenches of media or marketing, were photographers or video editors themselves, not just IT. Over time, agnostics understood the nature of DAM as opposed to DAS. These professionals can be found at DAM industry conferences such as Henry Stewart, NAB, MarTech, IBC, or CMSWire events.

Many companies have sprung up over the past few years that offer DAM initiatives far more capability than most organizations can appropriately fund. Here are some of the most common.

Metadata Curation

Everything in the past few chapters could be executed flawlessly, but without metadata curation, no initiative will succeed. While some organizations look to handle metadata entry through low level staff or even interns, quality metadata requires some expertise of the subject matter. To aid in this, several companies offer both remote and on site metadata entry and management. This is an excellent option for agencies or large firms that need both metadata management and library science expertise.

Rights Management Systems

Our digital conversation in marketing and media is instantly elevated with sports figures and celebrities. With the explosion of marketing channels and nearly any image as close as our nearest browser, companies are susceptible to copyright infringements like never before.

While any DAM system offers an ability to add rights metadata, organizations that use imagery, music or video will require a higher level of management to attach assets to contracts. These systems and service firms offer a robust way to manage the complexity of date, region, and other limitations that would be too expensive to manage manually. The potential legal fees and judgment awards of a single lawsuit will more than cover the cost of a DAM initiative and should be considered. These integrate directly with enterprise DAM systems and a few departmental ones. Research any judgments of this kind if possible.

Language Management Systems

In addition to offering interfaces in multiple localized languages, offering metadata in other languages can drive usage and adoption across the globe. Assuming the DAM system is able to manage to display a localized metadata field per user preferences, a value would be picked up by a language management system, translated and entered into the asset's specific language field. The translation itself is performed through primarily human means as electronic methods are, at this point, unreliable without significant expense.

System Integrators

There are also several large and boutique firms offering a variety of consulting, development, integration and training. Certain firms offer their own DAM systems along with these services. While not exactly agnostic, the level of DAM expertise is generally high in most respects.

DAM Vendors

A vendor in Digital Asset Management will endure long sales cycles, onerous Requests for Proposals, bad phone connections on critical demos, and opportunities that go dark for weeks. Although some are without a clue regarding DAM strategies, most are extremely knowledgeable about not only their products, but also DAM itself. Two in particular, Joel Warwick and Ed Durst, have continually impressed the industry with their knowledge of real world scenarios and how to ensure customer success.

How do we ensure we're considering the right vendor and technology? As stated before, from a features and technical standpoint, DAM requirements should be determined prior to contacting vendors to ensure that any proposed technical systems will support a legitimate need, not just something new. Without a proper analysis and list in place, fancy demonstrations can ensnare a program team into any sort of dangerous purchase.

To help sort this out, it's helpful to understand the different types of DAM vendors:

Enterprise DAM

This is an overused term that most vendors will use. True enterprise DAM systems will, among other capabilities, scale across many servers as needed without limit, handle custom metadata in specific models for specific users, provide a workflow engine, and offer options for user interfaces to ensure user adoption. There are only a handful of enterprise DAM vendors in the market today and we will continue to see more consolidation of these while smaller firms deliver enterprise type functionality.

What's unique about enterprise DAM vendors is the ability to scale and offer support for a wide variety of asset types and media supply chains far beyond storing any asset. Many support most needs for managing photography, graphics, some video, InDesign and other workflow needs. No packaged software vendor will align to all of a company's DAM needs with complete accuracy, but the ability to configure a feature rich system, rather than create custom forks in the code, is generally my recommendation. Enterprise DAM systems will, on average, deliver an ability to handle new needs, assets, workflows and users as they evolve over time. These systems provide a place for the organization to grow into, rather than hit a wall of capability that provokes users to find another way or program teams to seek out new systems.

Departmental DAM

These are generally designed for a specific workflow or asset type such as marketing, photography or video. Many are hosted in a cloud environment while others still offer an on premise option. While certainly capable, these systems are cheaper alternatives to an enterprise system and are often are chosen by teams looking to solve a DAM puzzle for their department. This is not to say that this is a poor choice, but if the decision is made in a silo, odds are the result will be as well.

Many of these systems are, at their core, "visual folders" without many fundamental features. Departmental DAM systems make perfect sense for a team that has a specific workflow that is too specific for an enterprise package. An example of this is a high resolution video MAM system that functions as an extension of a post production editorial process. Certain assets can then be sent to an enterprise DAM for general use. Another may be a photography system for soliciting secured talent approval. Selected shots can be sent to an enterprise DAM for additional metadata curation and collaboration.

A governance team should, through its research and recommendations, explain how a departmental DAM will integrate with other systems and even with a separate enterprise DAM system as needed.

Avoiding "RFP Hell"

Most program teams begin to construct the Request for Proposal (or Request for Quote) or RFP. The DAM requirements list within the business case is important to weed through the options, determine the needs, and avoid selecting the wrong technology or vendor. But it's also an item by which an initiative can get bogged down in "RFP Hell."

If properly developed, the list will contain many standard DAM features and a few items pertaining to a company's unique asset type, workflow, delivery need or integration. Some capabilities should be "make or break" non-negotiable items and bear more weight than say, an ability to generate a low resolution preview (which all legitimate DAM systems do).

In fact, if one is considering an enterprise DAM, since all

enterprise DAM systems do nearly the same things, asking for certain items is a waste of time. They all have their unique DNA and distinctions for a particular use. But listing out superfluous information in an RFP wastes an incredible amount of time for everyone. I have seen and worked on RFPs that have 400 lines of features of which 98% are in every enterprise DAM system. Although these are important features, program teams can spend hours investigating and debating something obvious. It's akin to asking if the sky is blue.

The trouble is most program teams develop their RFPs in either an IT vacuum, or have gone through what I call a "divining strategy." The IT vacuum occurs when an RFP is concerned with making distinctions between vendors such as in the case of shopping for firewalls or servers.

These RFPs list features, support, company information, and back office details, but fail to outline what users want and ultimately base their decision. Program teams follow this lead by shoehorning their strategic needs into lines within a spreadsheet. This fails to adequately communicate the spirit of the strategy or unique needs.

Without much more than a couple lines of description, vendors are forced to "divine" what's really needed. Vendors have poor divining powers and are boxed in with few opportunities to understand the real needs. Through cryptic emails or a conference call with all other vendors, they remain or are kicked out based on how well they can “divine” what the customer really wants.

Creating, answering and reviewing these documents can be a time consuming challenge for all involved, but especially vendors. RFPs can be excruciating. RFPs take one or two days to complete to achieve a satisfactory level for most customers. Most RFPs have impossible deadlines, sometimes only a few days. As a result, most DAM vendors will answer YES to nearly every item just to get through it. The rationale is most DAM systems today use open standards and are either configurable or customizable with an ample budget, so the thought is to say yes to all of it. As Obi-wan said, “It’s the truth, from a certain point of view.”

It’s not that vendors don’t care or are dishonest, but they don’t want to get kicked out of the process due to a lack of divination skills. So they say yes in the hope of having their day to make their case.

Given this abundance of vendor optimism and a good interface, a program team will be drawn to whatever system appeals to them and their budget in spite of any other issues. The RFP process is clearly broken. There are ways for customers and vendors to work more effectively so everyone can get on with it.

A better approach is to create “Mini RFIs" which lead to a simplified RFP. These are based on the research conducted by the program team and the go live needs. For these to be effective, a program team will need to disclose, among other functional group specific items, certain basic information:

1. The number of Power Users at go live and annual increases
2. The number of Casual Users at go live and annual increases
3. An estimate of the concurrent users at peak times
4. An estimate of the number of assets and storage needed
5. Unusual needs or workflows (one needs to know first what is unusual for a DAM system)

The IT RFI

This provides an IT oriented questionnaire that covers all aspects of the framework, storage strategy, server requirements, hosting options and all other technical details. It should be specific enough to identify any areas of concern and followed up by a phone call unless something is obvious. The IT team should provide for a score based on it's company policy and direction. Like technical metadata, this information is rather hard coded. A DAM system either works in .NET or something else. It's hosted in the cloud or on premise or can be both. It has proper archive storage hierarchies or it doesn't. Security options are wide, but there are best practices. Is it possible that the industry can standardize a technical questionnaire based on what is generally in popular use for all DAM vendors to pre-populate? If a vendor is being seriously considered, this RFI can be sent to a vendor and be returned, without being baked into 300 other lines and an unreasonable deadline, before more serious evaluations are made.

The Legal RFI

In many cases, software license agreements, statements of work, Master Services Agreements or even Non-Disclosure Agreements can cause incredible delays and even scuttle a purchase. Among the "heretofore and whereby's" within these agreements, a company will have policies that are either non-negotiable or standard. A brief, legal RFI can outline these requirements and offset the delays or problems later. Having the major items already identified weeks earlier, a line by line review can be scheduled immediately once a vendor is selected.

The Procurement RFI

This RFI provides a vendor a streamlined way to outline their pricing for licenses, services, and options for budgetary purposes. For the most part, vendors will be hesitant to provide this without the above information. However, they should be reminded that the information in a Procurement RFI is the same in any RFP.

Within this request, costs for the following should be sought:

1. Core, Development or other Server
2. User Licensing Structure
3. Optional Plug-ins or additional features

4. The number of servers required based on the above load and any licensing policies
5. An estimate of standard installation
6. Estimate of Configuration based on typical projects
7. Hosting options and storage tiers
8. Transfer acceleration options
9. Maintenance (expect 18-20% of licensing costs)
10. Additional phone support options
11. Any typically purchased or recommended options

The Business RFI

This RFI allows for the business to illustrate what is important to achieve the minimal viable product at go-live and for future needs. Instead of a long list of features, describe any non-negotiable items and primary workflows in detail, including specific tasks or integrations. Ask a vendor to describe how their system manages it (with screenshots where possible and/ or a description of how it is accomplished). Request they discuss their basic DAM functionality. The vendor should make it clear where any customization would be required or additional systems or options. Based on the answers you receive, select the top candidates (typically fewer than five) and make arrangements for an online demo.

Narrowing the field

With much of the background information reviewed or at hand, it's time to focus on the actual solution. It's helpful to organize these demos to reduce the amount of marketing spin. While beneficial, the focus should be on the system offered and functionality specific to the program's real world issues. Therefore, ensure the vendor adheres to a schedule such as this:

Introduction and vendor overview	30 Minutes
System Overview	30 Minutes
Primary Capabilities per Request	30 Minutes
Q&A	30 Minutes

Once demos are accomplished, the team must reduce the number of options to two or three vendors. At this point, it's strongly advised to work with the vendors to create working proofs of concept using actual company assets and workflows. A DAM vendor may require a fee for this. Given the stakes in getting this right, a few thousand dollars spent to work up a viable "sandbox" could be well worth it. This will also hold a program team accountable to spend a preliminary budget wisely and may help to focus the decision. This sandbox should have very specific objectives, but bear in mind that advanced workflows or complex metadata models may require high levels of effort to create. The goal is to prove certain concepts actually exist and provide a general understanding of administering and using the system.

The Open House Model

Once a sandbox has been created, the program team should invite stakeholders and users to a day long "open house" designed to provide a chance to review the system at their convenience. Presentations are helpful if the teams which gathered for workshops return as a group. This brings the initiative to a state of reality for those that worked hard to develop the business case. In some cases, individuals with concerns about the initiative or pending system may want to talk one on one. It's often the case where some users won't speak up in larger groups.

It's important that these users aren't forgotten or any anxiety may turn into system abandonment. Make a list of all stakeholders or users that attend these open houses and reach out to any that don't. Obviously it's imperative to have a trained user as a constructive guide during these discussions or personal demos.

And Then There Were Two

As the selection process proceeds, reduce the total number of vendors in contention to two. Your team should discuss the components of the system, the costs, technical aspects, interfaces, and implementation needs. The goal is to have a primary choice and a secondary. Finalize the actual needs of the minimal viable product required for go live and create a formal RFP. The next phase is negotiating the true costs with the vendor. Hopefully the team has had procurement and legal review the vendor from their perspective.

The reason for having two selected vendors is to have a backup in case any negotiations come to an impasse. Many vendors have been kicked out due to legal wrangling or a refusal to sign an actual Master Services or Software

Agreement. As the team should have requested, reviewed and agreed to these during the early stages of vendor engagement, this should have been already resolved. Having signatures on RFI response documents is always helpful in a conflict.

As your team and procurement finalize the true costs, go back to the business case and enter these figures into your worksheet and executive presentations. Schedule a meeting with your governance teams and walk them through the costs and refined project plan. The plan and recommended primary and secondary vendors, upon review, should be signed off by each governance team. Once the plan is signed off, schedule a meeting with the executive signatory for submission to the budget review process.

Let the selected vendors know they are in the final two. They will call you everyday to ask about status and what can be done to ensure a sale. Sometimes a scheduled 2-minute call with each by the program lead may calm them down.

Assuming the proposal is sound, there is still a chance it could be turned down. If things are not looking good, maintain communication with executives and governance teams to work out any issues if possilbe. It may not be the year for DAM, but persistence pays. For now, we'll assume the program team has approval to move forward.

...

11 FROM PUZZLE TO PICTURE

Implementation

Upon sign-off, acceptance and initial payment, the program team and vendor will outline the plan for technical delivery of the system. An internal IT project manager and a separate project manager from the business side is absolutely essential. No project of this nature will emerge successfully solely based on external resources or without a business project manager. The business side will be concerned with change management, organizational development and community-building. The program office will communicate and establish company best practices, policies and guidelines as well as participate in the technical updates.

A Phased Approach

The overall initiative will be divided into at least three phases from Phase 0 to Phase 2. Within Phase 0, the implementation team would likely focus on getting the environment and software commissioned. Other phases may include additional on-boarding, individual enhancement projects or upgrades. Bugs should be documented by the help desk or content services and both should have access to any issues reported by users or developers.

Phase 0

1. Hosting, storage and network infrastructure
2. Network connections to the hosted, managed facility
3. Installation of the core DAM application
4. Network Security
5. Integrate Single Sign-On

Phase 1

1. Configure preferences and personalization options
2. Planning and configuration of roles, security policies, user groups
3. Support escalation and ticketing system inclusion
4. Refine taxonomy and baseline controlled vocabularies, implementation and testing of metadata schema
5. Implementation of search strategy
6. Implementation of workflow processes

7. Existing asset migration
8. Provisioning, on-boarding and training of initial users
9. Planning for integration with other systems in Phase 2

Phase 2

1. Integration with ancillary systems
2. On-boarding and training of additional users
3. Planning for additional phases of expansion, integration and users

The implementation will follow a standard process of design, development, testing, migration, training, launch and support. It's critical to work with procurement and the IT department to ensure delivery of any required hardware as these may take weeks or months to acquire, set up and certify as ready.

Design

Within this portion, plans for the configuration of the software and technical infrastructure will be completed. Here is where the work during workshops pays off to reduce the amount of time and expense. As much as six weeks has been shaved off of a design phase for some deployments. The future states of workflows, metadata, taxonomies, user groups and roles, and interface requirements can be used as guides in this portion.

Development

Within the development portion, the program team will monitor the progress of the configuration of the system. Some companies use an agile development methodology which will introduce a host of technical management. These may include a project manager, technical lead, SCRUM master, business analyst, and developers. Where this methodology is enforced, expect to add additional budget line items. The teams will configure the DAM software on a development server, while meticulously hardening the production system. At a minimum, the infrastructure should consist of a production environment or a server for all users, and a development system, used for testing usage, enhancements and updates.

For greater confidence, flexibility and testing of new features or versions, a backup server, quality assurance (QA) and test servers should also be deployed. A QA server would have the exact server count and configuration as the production environment while test and development might use a single virtualized server. It's recommended to have complete access to these servers to adjust or test new configurations but only by trained developers. Some hosting sites or vendors do not allow sufficient development, test and QA servers and this will hinder future options by the program team.

At certain points during the configuration, sections of the system will be available for review by the team. As these are approved, the system will expand in functionality and this should generate a growing interest by everyone. Development updates are an exciting part of the weekly program and governance team meetings. As new features are configured, these can be communicated through the program office. Once the system has met its functional goals, it's ready for testing.

Testing

There are several testing plans needed by the program and technical teams at different times. Once the system is ready for more general functional testing, the program team and certain users will conduct User Acceptance Testing (UAT) under the guidance of the development team and DAM practitioner. It's common for the DAM consultant or practitioner to develop the UAT test plan using screen shots and a list of actions to perform. While these screens and actions should be in a document, it's helpful to use a tool such as Survey Monkey to provide a flexible method for distribution, test results, support tips, and updates.

IT will test the network, storage, server availability, operating system and security infrastructure. A load test is an automated method for simulating a number of users accessing the system concurrently. If the system breaks because fifty users all download a collection of assets all at once, it's better to know that prior to go live. Load testing systems are available in both commercial and open source applications.

Migration

If an organization is moving from the DAS world into DAM, it's likely there will be a multitude of disconnected repositories in place. Migrating these assets and whatever metadata exists will take special planning and work. It's been discussed in earlier chapters about establishing a master metadata schema and that will now be used. Existing metadata must be mapped into the DAM system using this schema. Various methods exist to move metadata and linked media files into a system. These include hot folder import and bulk loading scripts. Essentially these work through an XML or other specially formatted document and the asset(s) referenced within them, and copied into a network folder. The system runs a script every few minutes or hours and creates a new asset.

Typically, the media files and metadata must be imported concurrently or the script will fail. Scripting can be very tricky when used for migration or automatic import and requires an advanced knowledge of the system. Migration of thousands or even millions of assets can take a very long time depending on the method used.

Training

A training plan can be derived from the test plan in many cases. Rather than use canned vendor training manuals, it's recommended to develop custom training manuals, quick reference guides, and videos. Pre-packaged vendor training manuals may not look like the DAM system deployed, nor will the functionality it demonstrates be the same to your users.

Training is a critical point in the user adoption process and it can't be minimized. Placing these videos and other materials on internal support knowledge bases or even the DAM system itself is a powerful way for users to get familiar with the operation.

It's a common practice for companies to use a "train the

trainer" or remote screen share for training. This will not have the same level of user benefit as in person sessions. I have never seen it work well. There are hundreds of DAM scenarios that could be discussed that users will need. While corporate trainers are qualified for conducting educational sessions on systems such as email or Excel, they lack the experience of a DAM practitioner, especially when discussing the nuances of version control or XMP.

To estimate your training needs, assume at least 4-8 hours for each power user, 16 hours for an administrator, 5-10 days for an internal developer. Casual read only users should not require training at all.

Ongoing training for new power users will always be required. It's a good idea, in addition to end user group meetings and monthly training open houses, to record "snack sized" tips and tricks videos or conduct online training webinars and post them on the front page of the DAM system or through an internally accessed training portal.

Soft Launch

As the configuration and testing work is completed within the environments, users are trained, the system will be ready for launch. The help desk and content services teams should have been trained and updated on any risks of trouble. It's recommended to have a soft launch at least a week prior to any advertised go live date for certain users. At this point the team will have an excellent opportunity to test how effective its training and change management was.

DAS oriented systems or shared folders in use by this initial user group should be switched to a read only for these groups. As other groups may use these same systems, they should not be switched off entirely but this change may bring about chaos if not communicated and managed well. Any bugs or issues encountered by this soft launch group should be attended to with "hyper care" to ensure a high level of support.

Launch

As part of the rollout plan, the same soft launch strategy and activities will be used. Casual users will be redirected from any existing DAMs and Power Users will use the DAM system exclusively where possible. The support and content services teams are now the main face of the system to the user and should continually monitor issues, complaints, or any opportunities. Any new assets not migrated will have to be brought in.

Communicating with all stakeholders en masse upon launch is a two edged sword. On the one side, it's exciting to let everyone know the DAM system is launched. On the other side, it may create such as massive load beyond any reasonable estimate of concurrent users the servers may crash. A new user finding the system unavailable or slow at first access may never return to it. Communication to stakeholder groups should therefore be done on off peak times and the team should monitor the load. Once the load trends are understood, broader communication can be made to provide updates and maintain awareness.

Start Small, Check, then Grow

As the system continues to operate and roll out, its recommended to check in with the stakeholder and user groups that were part of the earlier research. This is helpful to understand if the proposed optimized workflows are delivering the experience and efficiency hoped for. Are searches actually returning the expected results? Are there bugs or work arounds that create more work? This check along with system reporting will be important to bring back to the governance teams.

In addition to common reports such as a weekly count of downloads and uploads, it's also helpful to know:

1. The number of unique user log ins
2. The most commonly used search terms (helps to understand what users want)
3. A list of the number and kind of assets in the system
4. The number of users from different offices or geographies
5. Any assets created in one geography that are used by another

Deploying a server with DAM software is challenging, but it pales in comparison to getting users to accept and prefer it over folders and loose hard drives. Change management is the hardest part of DAM initiatives especially when the options for storing and delivery are switch off. Proper ongoing governance, training and communication are essential for ensuring your DAM puzzle doesn't break up into pieces again.

...

12 EXPANDING THE BORDERS

DAM is a Road, Not a Destination

Upon launch and acceptance by stakeholders, a company shifts from survival to a state of digital transformation. At certain points, users and executives will realize the power of DAM and begin to think differently. Then this realization will transform into expectation. If users are properly and continually on-boarded through communication, governance and accept the initiative's system, these shifts to more flexibility and capability will be painless compared to the digital survival previously endured. Teams will operate not in the manually driven, folder and file naming world, but within a collaborative, efficient and digitally mature manner. The feature requests will be more ambitious and groups will come up with ideas and solutions that will surprise the program team. It may take a year from launch for these small victories to occur, but they should happen.

The Party's Not Over

With the system launched, bugs and issues minimized, and as more users shift to the DAM platform, the governance teams may believe there is nothing left to do. While most technical applications such as email are more "launch, train and maintain," a DAM system is dynamic. Media files, workflows and delivery options are continually evolving and shifting and once an organization has made that shift, new opportunities to improve and refine emerge. How far the company will take this will depend on the new charter of the governance teams.

As noted before, the DAM governance teams should consider changing their designation to a Digital Governance team. This enhances the field of view and shifts the emphasis to a strategic direction. As a DAM governance team, the various groups and stakeholders learned how to work together and collaborate on a large, but entry level initiative toward digital maturity. It would be catastrophic to disband and lose that momentum. The future is too murky and ever changing to remain in digital transformation and the teams, given the chance, will uncover new opportunities previously inconceivable. The shift to a digital platform based on collaboration, efficiency and transparency allows the company to think and move beyond the borders of a DAM puzzle in simple to extraordinary ways. What could this look like for you?

1. Product imagery can be tagged with metadata to be automatically added to a sales collateral folder and delivered to sales enablement tools.
2. The integration of media creation, management, delivery and analytics to understand a customer journey, but predict it. This would analyze what is working in various geographies or markets. Workflows can automatically generate media creation requests and reduce the cycle time for new assets.
3. Asset elements, much like dynamic content, can be automatically combined into new creative assets tailored to a customer engagement.
4. Hundreds of Radio and TV commercials once managed by media distributors for a large fee can now be gathered within a company's DAM system. This reduces the management fees, ensures consistency from outside agencies, and provides a method to move to another distributor if needed.
5. Skip the media distributor all together and deliver commercials and metadata directly to networks and affiliates. Product imagery can be named with a product code and date stamp that the DAM system can use to look up and automatically enter basic information or make up to the minute changes.
6. With 3D printing maturing into the mainstream,

companies with CAD models for furniture, accessories or home goods may to sell these digital assets on demand for local delivery or even within a customer's home. A replica of a Ming Dynasty vase while you wait.

7. A brand may realize that after deploying a DAM system and digital governance, like all other major brands today, are actually a media company.

8. Executives will realize digital survival won't work anymore.

9. DAM is as familiar a phrase in business as "eCommerce.

10. You will realize DAM is a puzzle worth solving and you'll be successful in leading others in revolutionary DAM initiatives.

...

13 THE PIECES THAT DON'T FIT

The Lingering Pieces

Everyone's DAM puzzle is their own and no initiative is perfect. I've found it easier to remember what not to do by acknowledging when I'm doing it. As a means of concluding the key points of this book, here are 99 ways of ensuring your DAM initiative will fail (or be very limited).

Perhaps you'll use these to recognize if you or your team is starting to work ways that may not be helpful. Good Luck!

99 Ways Digital Asset Management Initiatives Fail

1. Start off by shopping for DAM technology
2. Assume that a DAM initiative doesn't require a business case
3. Don't consider DAM as a fundamental business strategy
4. Don't audit your asset types or their lifecycles
5. Don't review your workflows or stakeholders
6. Let your manual processes continue after you've deployed a DAM system
7. Don't measure, identify or estimate what DAM will do for you.
8. Don't consider all potential stakeholders
9. Don't benchmark your workflows against a future, optimized one
10. Expect to have DAM expertise already in house
11. Don't confirm business commitments or funding in advance.
12. Assume your users will use the system
13. Give your users lots of media conversion options when downloading
14. Don't brand your DAM platform
15. Expect all media asset types can be managed within a single DAM system
16. Allow alternative methods of storing and delivery
17. Don't get top executive level buy-in on the initiative
18. Don't create forums for issues and continuous improvement
19. Don't get funding commitments early for items such as

licensing fees, maintenance, consulting, professional services, hardware or hosting

20. Let the tech team handle it
21. Use SharePoint
22. Use Digital Asset Storage (DAS) practices
23. Don't appoint an internal project manager from the business side
24. Don't appoint an internal project manager from the IT side
25. Don't appoint a program team
26. Skip cross functional governance
27. Don't engage directors, vice presidents or designers
28. Expect your help desk to know why InDesign won't convert to a PDF
29. Don't create a Content Services team
30. Assume you are the governance
31. Assume governance is there primarily for dictating policy
32. Consider only your team's requirements.
33. Don't evaluate your near or far stakeholders
34. Try to "Boil the Ocean" and make your DAM system all things to everyone the first day
35. Just buy an application that manages content (web, print, etc)
36. Don't integrate metadata from other systems
37. Don't worry about change management
38. Don't have a plan for communication to stakeholders
39. Assume that after the system is launched, the hard part is over
40. Don't worry about aligning metadata
41. Consider DAM as a really smart hard drive

42. Don't conduct asset lifecycle and workflow audits
43. Train the Trainer
44. Use online meetings for training
45. Don't include your IT management
46. Buy something cheap until the real system is in place
47. Once the system is up and running, disband the governance teams
48. Expect success to magically happen
49. Expect user adoption to be successful
50. Create more work for creative teams than they had before

Don't create a business case

52. Don't worry about talking to a CFO prior to developing a business case
53. Use an archive management system to handle assets
54. Expect everyone to know what Digital Asset Management is in meetings
55. Continue to deliver smaller assets through email
56. Allow everyone to use the DAM system as an option
57. Don't use the DAM system to deliver to social media platforms
58. Create a single user interface for everyone to use
59. Force everyone to use the same long list of metadata fields
60. Ensure the system you choose creates multiple copies of the same asset
61. Call vendors before creating a DAM initiative, charter, and plan
62. Expect casual users to know how to use the system
63. Use the system for finished assets only
64. Don't measure user behavior on the system
65. Expect that a cloud system will handle high resolution

video

66. Upon launch, email the entire company to come take a look
67. Don't review legal agreements prior to selecting a vendor
68. Upon launch, immediately shut off all other means of storing or delivering assets
69. Expect the process of moving assets from existing repositories will be quick
70. Expect delivery of hardware to host your system will be as easy as ordering a new computer
71. Don't involve actual users in your user acceptance testing
72. Skip user acceptance testing entirely
73. Expect everyone to speak English
74. Don't have a backup choice when selecting a vendor
75. Expect a software maintenance fee to include phone support
76. Select a vendor on price and how pretty the user interface is
77. Create RFPs with hundreds of lines of requirements
78. Don't require a proof of concept sandbox for your users prior to a purchase
79. Don't train your users on the sandbox
80. Don't manage your users expectations when using the sandbox
81. Don't conduct open houses for your users to get comfortable with your progress
82. Don't conduct load testing on your system prior to launch
83. When launch day comes, make sure everyone can do everything they expect
84. Expect your vendor project manager to ensure your metadata is what your company really needs

85. Expect a vendor based consultant to care about your internal governance
86. Don't check in with executives frequently prior to submitting your business case
87. Don't worry about digital maturity
88. Expect that DAM is such a good idea that executives will fund immediately it
89. Ensure your department owns the DAM initiative
90. Ensure the tech team owns the DAM initiative
91. Use process improvement and cost reductions as the primary argument for DAM
92. Talk to only one person in a department to understand what's going on
93. Expect video editors to have the same needs as photographers
94. Assume everyone has the same workflows as you do
95. Don't worry about how the metadata will be curated and entered. Let someone else worry about it.
96. Expect searches to work as intuitively as Google
97. Make sure you have more than 10 required metadata fields
98. Buy what everyone else considers to be the best DAM system out there
99. Don't read this book

...

"We went from around $2M in annual rights management lawsuit penalties and fees to zero in less than 2 years."
- Director of Digital Operations for Fortune 500 company

DAM Industry Resources

DAM EDUCATION

The DAM Academy	damacademy.com
The DAM Foundation	damfoundation.org
Henry Stewart Events	damusers.com
Kings College London	www.kcl.ac.uk

EVENTS

AIIM Conference	aiimevents.com
Gilbane Conference	gilbane.com
Henry Stewart Events	damusers.com
IBC	ibc.org
MarTech Conference	martechconf.com
NAB	nabshow.org

PUBLICATIONS & REPORTS

JDDM	henrystewartpublications.com/jdmm
DAM Research	realstorygroup.com/Reports/DAM

The DAM ROI Factory

Department ABC Agency

Summary | Baseline | Systems | Costs

Hours per Week Communication Activities	Staff Present	Staff Future	Manager/Director Present	Manager/Director Future	Legal Present	Legal Future	Agency or Supplier Present	Agency or Supplier Future	Total Costs Present	Total Costs Future
Ideation	3	1							$45	$15
Produce									$0	$0
Ingest	5	1							$75	$15
Catalog	8	2							$120	$30
Search	8	2			15	2	16	4	$3165	$660
Edit							6	1	$720	$120
Repurpose/ Version	2	1							$30	$15
Transcode									$0	$0
Archive									$0	$0
Deliver *	12	2	4	0			10	2	$1480	$270
Update/Report			4	1			5	1	$700	$145
Train	1	0	1	0					$40	$0
Total Hours	39	9	9	1	15	2	37	8		

Hours/Week Other	System Labor/ Support/Maint Present	System Labor/ Support/Maint Future	Infrastructure Present	Infrastructure Future	Cycle Time Present	Cycle Time Future	Lost Opportunity Present	Lost Opportunity Future	Total Costs Present	Total Costs Future
14 Systems	.1		.1		.1				$133.14	$0
Brand Inconsistency									$0	$0
Marketing Abandonment									$0	$0

Estimated Existing Global Costs: $6,508.14/**Week**

Estimated Future Global Costs: $1,270/**Week**

Benefits: **$5,238.14 per Week** **$261,907 per Year**

Sample Workflow Diagram

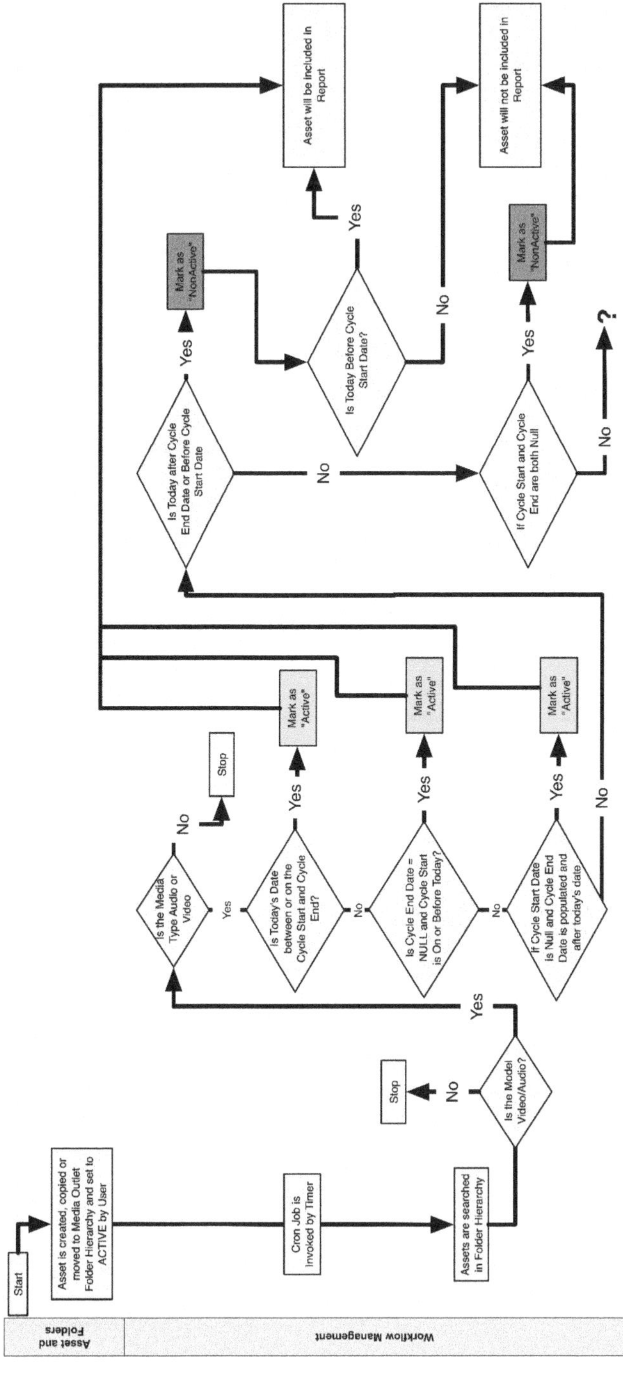

ACKNOWLEDGMENTS

There are many people I would like to thank for what is in this book. Some allowed me to tag along in their projects, others have been partners, and then there are friends with whom I've worked and learned. For those I consider my DAM friends, it would be impossible to list them all. But I would like to thank a few.

David Lipsey and Patricia Connolly are responsible for not only the Henry Stewart DAM Conferences, but also leading the industry in providing the best forums for case studies, practices and thought leadership in DAM. Thank you both. Much of any success I have is due to your support and generosity for more than a decade.

For those that allowed a neophyte DAM enthusiast to tag along and learn from the best, I'd like to thank Michael Moon, Jon Schupp, Katherine Parker, Linda Burman, Tim Padilla, Skiff Wager, Frank Chagoya, Dennis Pannuto, David Austerberry, and Adrian Scott. I would also like to thank Richard Eberhart for my pivotal opportunity to learn DAM by interviewing dozens of organizations between 2003-2006 for the Global Society for Asset Management—a group well ahead of its time.

Two people in particular of whom I have eternal respect and gratitude for is Charles Day and Chris Tardio of The Lookinglass Consultancy in New York. They believed in me during my early years in DAM and as the CTO for their one of a kind company.

Over the years, I've worked with some of the best media people, executives, consultants, organizations and creative minds in the business. We've shared in many media endeavors from when I was a production grunt to DAM coach. These are the leaders who greatly influenced me with their genius, advice, wisdom, friendship and encouragement: Alan Saporta, Alex Grossman, Angus Wallace, Annie Chang, Beth Goldstein, Brian Brightly, Carin Forman, Charles Rignall, Chris Whalen, Christina Aguilera, Conor Linberg, David Meisel, David Rolfe, Diane Burley, Eddie Drake, Emmelie Forsyth, George Grippo, Guy Hellier, Jason Bright, Jeff Boarini, Jess Hartmann, Jeff Heise, John Florence, John Smith, John Price, Jon Christian, Julia Ormond, Karen Chiacu, Leon Silverman,

Mark Davey, Markus Schumacher, Mary Yurkovic, Matt Thesing, Matthew Phillips, Michelle Bernheim, Mike Arnold, Nancy Baca, Neil Paton, Nish Patel, Paul Andersen, Paul Nicholson, Peggy Leyden, Randy Haberkamp, Rick Lawley, Rob Kobrin, Robin Parisse, Roe Bressan, Scott Marvel, Sir Peter Smithers, Srikanth Raghavan, Suanne McGrath-Kelly, Suzanne Van Dam, Theresa Regli, Tim Padilla, Tom Fletcher, Tony Lipria, Tracy Askam, Vince Roberts, Steve Winzenburg, and Woody Zwirn.

I'd also like to thank Kristin Petrovich Kennedy for her generous support and partnership to expand the DAM conversation and providing me with ways to share my views on DAM within a creative outlet. Finally, a special thanks to my good friends Paul Riggio, Brian Plante, and Colin Birch with whom I've shared many DAM adventures and look forward to many more.

ABOUT THE AUTHOR

Dan McGraw is a digital strategy coach with a passion to educate and create value through innovative strategies, technical insight, business expansion and creative enablement. His specialty is digital maturity and strategy, DAM and content management, post production and media workflow within the Advertising, Corporate, Motion Picture, Broadcast & Cable, and Print & Publishing fields. As a technology advisor, CTO, fractional executive, and consultant for over 20 years, he has developed strategies and solutions for McDonald's, Caterpillar, Disney, Avid, as well as many other corporations, non-profits, government, film/post facilities and advertising agencies. He can be reached via email at either danmcgraw@me.com or dan@solvingthedampuzzle.com.

PHOTO COURTESY OF JASON BRIGHT/MEDIABEACON

Lightning Source UK Ltd.
Milton Keynes UK
UKHW052110040219
336736UK00010B/285/P